Easy-Care Perennial Gardens

Easy-Care Perennial Gardens

Techniques and Plans for Beds and Borders You Can Grow and Enjoy

Plus: 10 Beautiful Garden Designs

Susan McClure

Rodale Press, Inc.
Emmaus, Pennsylvania

Our Purpose

"We inspire and enable people to improve their lives and the world around them"

Quarto Publishing Staff
Managing Editor: Sally MacEachern
Senior Editor: Louisa McDonnell
Editor: Sally Roth
Editorial Director: Mark Dartford
Indexer: Dorothy Frame
Senior Art Editor: Antonio Toma
Designer: Jessica Caws
Picture Researcher: Giulia Hetherington
Cover Designer: Penny Dawes
Interior Illustrators: Dick Barnard, Robin Griggs, Wayne Ford, Michelle Draycott
Art Director: Moira Clinch

Rodale Press Home and Garden Books Staff
Vice President and Editorial Director: Margaret J. Lydic
Managing Editor: Ellen Phillips
Editor: Fern Marshall Bradley
Copy Editor: Ann Snyder

If you have any questions or comments concerning the editorial content of this book, please write to:
    Rodale Press, Inc.
    Book Readers' Service
    33 East Minor Street
    Emmaus, PA 18098

Library of Congress Cataloging-in-Publication Data
McClure, Susan
    Easy-care perennial gardens: techniques and plans for beds and borders you can grow and enjoy
      p. cm.
      Includes bibliographical references (p.) and index.
      ISBN 0–87596–778–7 (hc : alk. paper)
      1. Perennials. 2. Landscape gardening. 3. Gardens—Design.
I. Title.
SB434.M364 1997
635.9'32——dc20   96-19375

Typeset in Great Britain by Central Southern Typesetters
Manufactured in Singapore by Universal Graphics Pte Ltd
Printed in Singapore by Star Standard Industries Pte Ltd

Distributed in the book trade by St. Martin's Press

2 4 6 8 10 9 7 5 3 1 hardcover

Contents

How to Use This Book

Once you begin planting perennials, you'll discover that they're true garden friends. Every spring, you can look forward to the pleasure of getting reacquainted as your perennials send up fresh green foliage and a dazzling display of flowers.

One of the best ways to enjoy perennials is in an easy-care perennial garden – one that looks wonderful, but takes minimal care. The secret to a successful and easy-care perennial garden is advance planning: choosing the right plants, preparing your site properly, and putting the plants together in a pleasing design. If you pay attention to these three basics, you can have a beautiful, easy-care garden. All the information you need to do just that is in this book.

Easy-Care Perennial Gardens has three parts, each of which can help you attain your goal of a beautiful easy-care perennial garden.

● If you'd like to browse through a potpourri of wonderful designs, any of which may be exactly what your yard needs, see "Easy-Care Garden Designs" beginning on page 8. If you have a sunny site in mind, turn to the Intriguing Island Bed on page 16, the Color Theme Gardens on page 22, or the Colonial Cottage Garden on page 40. Nature lovers should turn to the Butterfly and Hummingbird Garden on page 52. For a design that includes roses, check out the Romantic Perennial, Herb, and Rose Garden on page 34 and the Dynamic Driveway Border on page 46.

Perhaps you need a design for a shaded site. You'll find ideas in A Perennial Foundation Planting on page 10 and A Fabulous Four-Season Garden on page 64. For a shady garden under trees, consider A Serene Shade Garden on page 28 and A Wonderful Wildflower Garden on page 58.

When you find a design you like, be sure to turn to the following page. There you'll find garden options – suggestions for changing garden sizes or color schemes, or substituting sun plants for shade.

● Before you embark on planting your garden, you need to know what it takes to grow perennials. Consult "Easy-Care Basics" starting on page 70. It covers all the techniques for perennial growing, from soil preparation and choosing plants to propagation and pest control.

● You'll need the details on caring for specific perennials after you've planted your garden, whether you use a design from this book or your own design. The "Easy-Care Perennial Encyclopedia" beginning on page 92 covers 60 terrific perennials. You'll find descriptions of the best easy-care species and cultivars, suggestions on how to use and combine the plants in gardens, and special tips on the kind of site and care each plant needs to look its best.

There's nothing more satisfying than a successful perennial garden. Each year, it returns looking better than the year before. With *Easy-Care Perennial Gardens*, you're guaranteed success. Your only problem may be deciding *which* wonderful perennial garden you want to try first!

▶ **Yellow coreopsis** and red crocosmias are a colorful duo for an easy-care perennial garden.

Easy-Care Garden Designs

There's nothing as beautiful as a carefully designed perennial garden. You see them in glossy photos in magazines and books and wonder how you could ever have a garden as gorgeous as that. Actually, there's a trick that makes it possible for anyone to have a beautiful garden filled with colorful perennials. The trick is to start with a good design, then use tough, easy-care perennials that don't need a lot of pampering to look their best. To show you just how great looking easy-care perennials can be, I got together with three other perennial garden designers to create ten exciting and fun perennial gardens. To start with, designers Alexander Apanius, Robin Siktberg, Bobbie Schwartz, and I chose many of our favorite easy-care perennials — plants with beautiful blooms, attractive foliage and form, and the ability to thrive simply if given the right amount of sun or shade and reasonably decent soil.

We settled on a reliable cast of 60 easy-care perennials, plus a few additional plants for special situations. Then we came up with layouts for traditional and innovative perennial gardens for all kinds of yards and both big and little spaces. You're sure to find a garden – or several! – that's perfect for you.

Each design illustrates how to pair up compatible plants, develop a sequence of bloom, and combine plants with different heights, textures, and flower colors to create a satisfying garden. I've also suggested ways to adapt each garden to add your own personality. I'll show you how to change the length, width, color, and more to customize the design to your yard. Finally, each garden includes a project – something you can make or do to make your garden even more beautiful and enjoyable.

With the great designs you'll find here, any time is a good time to start thinking about and planning a perennial garden!

A PERENNIAL FOUNDATION PLANTING

*If the foundation of your house is a victim of sad-shrub syndrome,
treat it to a perennial makeover. Drifts of beautiful easy-care perennials can make the most ordinary
foundation planting something special. The perennials soften the stark form of woody plants and bring a
riot of spring and summer color to brighten the front of your house.*

This Perennial Foundation Planting fits comfortably on the north side of a single-story ranch or two-story colonial home. Landscaping a north-facing home can be a challenge because of the mix of sun and shade conditions. This planting rises to the challenge with a mix of sun- and shade-loving perennials. Perennials for light shade cluster near the house, while perennials for sun grow in island beds. A vine-clad trellis stretches up the wall beside a picture window. This design makes a beautiful finished picture, but if it seems too elaborate to tackle all at once, try breaking out just a few of the beds to plant. Or, rework the plan to fit the shape and exposure of your house, as described on pages 12 and 13.

▼ **A mix of evergreen shrubs** makes a wonderful backdrop for the easy-care perennials in this foundation planting. Sweeps of moss phlox and Persian epimedium are just one of the many wonderful flowering combinations that this foundation garden offers.

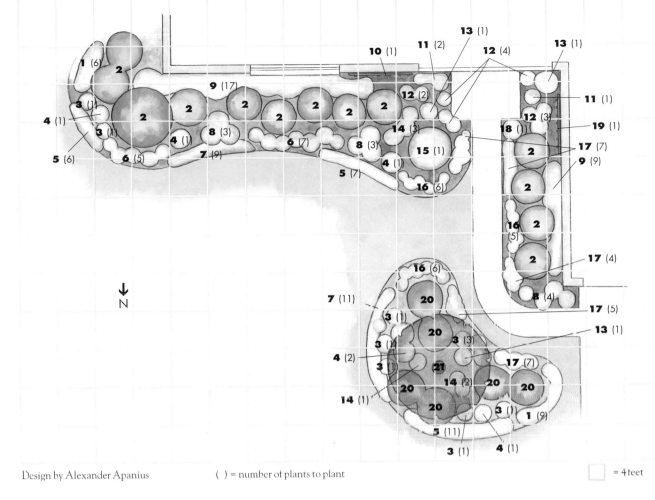

Design by Alexander Apanius   ( ) = number of plants to plant   ☐ = 4 feet

The Planting Plan. Many of the plants in the Perennial Foundation Planting will spread as they grow, reducing or eliminating weeding. Because their topgrowth dies back during winter, these perennials won't suffer damage if heavy loads of snow cascade off the roof. None of the perennials in this planting need staking, and all are virtually pest-free. The island bed at the curve of the entry walk is optional. The Sargent's weeping hemlock is a small tree with overlapping arching branches. It does best in moist soil and will eventually reach 10 feet tall. See page 15 for more information on clematis vines.

1 'Sulphureum' Persian epimedium (*Epimedium* x *versicolor* 'Sulphureum')

2 Existing shrubs

3 'Zagreb' threadleaf coreopsis (*Coreopsis verticillata* 'Zagreb')

4 'Happy Returns' daylily (*Hemerocallis* 'Happy Returns')

5 Mixed blue-, pink-, and white-flowered moss phlox (*Phlox subulata*)

6 'Wargrave Pink' Endress cranesbill (*Geranium endressii* 'Wargrave Pink')

7 'Tricolor' two-row sedum (*Sedum spurium* 'Tricolor') with Siberian squill (*Scilla siberica*)

8 'Sprite' star astilbe (*Astilbe simplicifolia* 'Sprite')

9 Lily-of-the-valley (*Convallaria majalis*)

10 Pink anemone clematis (*Clematis montana* var. *rubens*)

11 Siberian bugloss (*Brunnera macrophylla*)

12 'Roy Davidson' lungwort (*Pulmonaria* 'Roy Davidson')

13 'So Sweet' hosta (*Hosta* 'So Sweet')

14 'Luxuriant' bleeding heart (*Dicentra* 'Luxuriant')

15 Sargent's weeping hemlock (*Tsuga canadensis* 'Pendula')

16 'Chatterbox' coral bells (*Heuchera* x *brizoides* 'Chatterbox')

17 'Bronze Beauty' ajuga (*Ajuga reptans* 'Bronze Beauty') with 'Tête-à-Tête' daffodil (*Narcissus* 'Tête-à-Tête')

18 Christmas rose (*Helleborus niger*)

19 'Henryi' clematis (C. 'Henryi')

20 Creeping junipers

21 Japanese maple

STARTING FROM SCRATCH

Sometimes foundation shrubs like yews get so overgrown they just aren't right for the site anymore. They cover window views or block walkways. Your best choice may be to cut them down and start over. Or, if you've bought a new house, it may not have a foundation planting at all.

If you decide to lay your foundation bare before planting the Perennial Foundation Planting (or if you live in a newly built home that isn't landscaped), here are some well-behaved woody plants that will work well in the design:

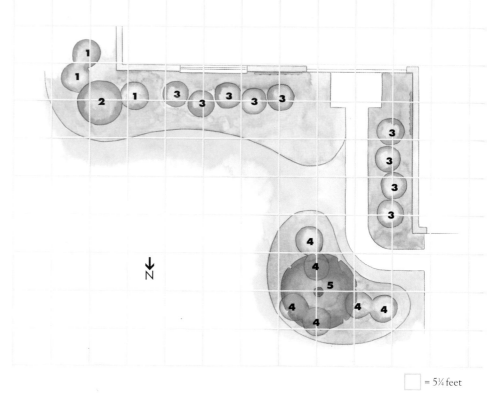

= 5¼ feet

1 'Nordic' inkberry (*Ilex glabra* 'Nordic')

2 'Shasta' doublefile viburnum (*Viburnum plicatum* 'Shasta')

3 'Nova Zembla' rhododendron (*Rhododendron* 'Nova Zembla')

4 'Blue Pacific' shore juniper (*Juniperus conferta* 'Blue Pacific')

5 'Bloodgood' Japanese maple (*Acer palmatum* 'Bloodgood')

'Nordic' inkberry: Shiny, deep green leaves are the strong point of this holly relative. It grows 3 to 4 feet tall and wide.

'Shasta' doublefile viburnum: This viburnum has very large white flowers and lovely reddish purple fall foliage. It reaches 6 feet tall and 10 feet wide when mature.

'Nova Zembla' rhododendron: This heat-tolerant rhododendron sports dark red flowers. It grows to 5 feet tall and wide.

'Blue Pacific' shore juniper: A low-growing juniper with silver-blue foliage that spreads slowly to form a dense mat.

'Bloodgood' Japanese maple: The graceful form and intense red, finely cut leaves make this Japanese maple a must. It will grow slowly to reach 12 to 15 feet tall.

All of these shrubs are hardy in Zones 5 through 9.

Whenever you're shopping for trees or shrubs, always check with your supplier about hardiness, soil requirements, and light requirements *before* you buy to save yourself from an expensive mistake.

MORE SHRUB CHOICES Of course, the shrubs listed above aren't the only ones you can use in the Perennial Foundation Planting. You may want to check the selection at local garden centers and nurseries and choose your own just-right shrubs. Or, pick from the following to substitute for the shrubs named above.

Inkberry alternatives: Mountain laurel (*Kalmia latifolia*) gives a beautiful floral display in spring and has excellent evergreen foliage. Try a mix of pink-flowered cultivars in place of inkberry, but keep in mind that mountain laurel requires cool, acid, moist, well-drained soil to grow well. Another evergreen alternative is 'Green Gem' hybrid boxwood (*Buxus* 'Green Gem'), which produces low mounds of dense dark green foliage.

Viburnum alternatives: Fragrant viburnum (*Viburnum carlesii*), which has delightfully scented white flowers, is an excellent choice for backyard gardens. You could also try 'Pink Princess' weigela (*Weigela florida* 'Pink Princess'), a prolific bloomer that produces bright pink flowers in spring. Purple-leaved sand cherry (*Prunus* x *cistena*) has pink flowers and attractive bronze leaves.

Rhododendron alternatives: If bright red flowers aren't to your taste, try white-flowered 'Album' Catawba rhododendron (*Rhododendron catawbiense* 'Album') or 'Roscum Elegans' rhododendron (*R.* 'Roseum Elegans'), a fast-growing, rounded shrub with lilac-rose blooms.

Shore juniper alternatives: Some cultivars of yew are excellent foundation plants. One of the best is the elegant, low-growing 'Repandens' English yew (*Taxus baccata* 'Repandens').

Japanese maple alternatives: Paperbark maple (*Acer griseum*) grows up to 12 feet tall and 15 feet wide and has cinnamon-brown peeling bark for year-round interest. Amur maple (*A. ginnala*) grows 15 to 18 feet tall and wide, has colorful fall foliage, and is extremely hardy (to Zone 2). Sourwood (*Oxydendrum arboreum*) has brilliant fall color. It is a slow-growing tree (to 15 feet in 15 years), but eventually can grow to 50 feet tall. Use a multistemmed type for mixed plantings. White fringe tree (*Chionanthus virginicus*) grows to 30 feet tall and has loose clusters of white flowers that mature to blue grapelike fruit on the female trees. Pagoda dogwood (*Cornus alternifolia*) has white flowers and blue-black fruit; it reaches 20 feet tall and 12 feet wide.

◀ **For a shady foundation planting,** rely on hostas to add interesting leaf color and texture. Try combining them with evergreen shrubs. A favorite garden ornament can also give your foundation garden that special touch.

BUILDING A TRELLIS It's easy to make a rectangular trellis like the ones used in the Perennial Foundation Planting. Each trellis is 6 feet wide and 5 feet high with a grid pattern.

You will need:

- 11 5-foot-long cedar 1 x 2s
- 9 6-foot-long cedar 1 x 2s
- 115 #6 x 1½-inch stainless steel screws
- Stain or paint
- 2 57-inch-long 2 x 4s
- 2 6-foot-long 2 x 4s
- 8 16d galvanized nails
- 2 8-foot-long 4 x 4 posts
- 8 #8 x 3-inch stainless steel screws
- Electric drill

1 Lay out the cedar strips on a level driveway, patio, or garage floor. Arrange the 5-foot-long strips (the vertical 1 x 2s) first. Then lay the 6-foot strips on top of them to form a grid. The openings in the grid should be about 6 inches square.

2 Predrill a ³⁄₃₂-inch hole in each junction of the strips. Then screw the strips together with stainless steel screws.

3 Set the trellis upright against a wall, and stain or paint the trellis to match the color of your house.

4 On a level surface, lay out the 2 x 4s on edge to make a rectangular frame for the trellis. Nail the 2 x 4s together with 16d galvanized nails, two per corner.

5 Lay the trellis on the frame. Predrill holes in the left and right sides of the trellis through to the frame. Make holes in the vertical strips only. Screw the trellis to the frame.

6 Erect two 4 x 4 posts 5 feet apart at the location in your garden where you plan to plant vines. Sink about 2½ feet of the posts into the ground, leaving about 5½ feet above ground.

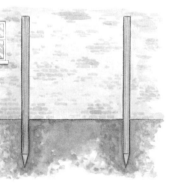

7 Stand the trellis upright against the posts, with the 2 x 4s touching the posts. Use scrap lumber to raise the trellis about 4 inches off the ground. Drive two 3-inch stainless steel screws at an angle through the upper face of the top 2 x 4 into each post. Then repeat at the bottom, driving the screws at an angle through the lower face of the bottom 2 x 4.

◀ **Bold clematis** flowers and trumpet-shaped goldflame honeysuckle blossoms make a great late summer combination for a sunny trellis.

GROWING VINES ON TRELLISES Perennial vines have long twining or clinging stems that require a little special care. Vines that twine or hang by tendrils, such as clematis and porcelain vine, require support and tend to stay put on a trellis. Others, such as Boston ivy, Virginia creeper, and wintercreeper, can cling to and climb many surfaces, including your house and your shrubs. They may spread to cover a wider area than you planned unless you prune them vigorously. Feel free to thin out old or crowded growth or remove aggressively spreading sections. Time pruning of flowering vines so you don't cut off all the flower buds. For summer-flowering vines like honeysuckle, prune in late winter to early spring. Some types of clematis flower in spring, others in summer. Their pruning requirements are a little more specialized, so ask your supplier for specific pruning directions for the type of clematis you're buying. For more information on vine care, see "Recommended Reading" on page 155.

VINES FOR A SUNNY TRELLIS Here are some great vines for a foundation garden in sun or light shade, such as the north side of a single-story ranch or sunny east, west, or south exposures of a ranch or taller house.

Five-leaf akebia (*Akebia quinata*): This vine's brownish purple flowers are not showy, but they are fragrant. They are followed by purple berries on vines up to 40 feet.

Goldflame honeysuckle (*Lonicera* x *heckrottii*): Reddish purple trumpet-shaped flowers with yellow interiors open from summer into fall on these vines, which grow from 10 to 25 feet.

Pink anemone clematis (*Clematis montana* var. *rubens*): Abundant light pink flowers with vanilla fragrance appear on this clematis in early summer. Vines can reach 30 feet.

Porcelain vine (*Ampelopsis brevipedunculata*): Porcelain vine sports clusters of pea-sized berries that change from lilac to porcelain blue in fall.

'Superba Jackmanii' clematis (*Clematis* 'Superba Jackmanii'): This clematis has large, handsome, violet-blue flowers that appear in late summer on vines up to 20 feet.

Sweet autumn clematis (*Clematis maximowicziana*): This vigorous grower reaches up to 30 feet. It has fragrant white flowers in late summer and early fall that mature into attractive seedheads.

VINES FOR A SHADED TRELLIS These vines are perfect for foundation gardens on the north side of two-story homes.

'Lowii' Boston ivy (*Parthenocissus tricuspidata* 'Lowii'): This cultivar has three-lobed ivylike leaves. It is similar to Virginia creeper but grows more slowly. It also has spectacular red fall color.

Virginia creeper (*Parthenocissus quinquefolia*): The five-lobed leaves, which turn brilliant red in fall, are the best feature of this vine, which can grow to 40 feet.

Wintercreeper (*Euonymus fortunei*): This glossy-leaved evergreen comes in a showy variegated form and can grow to 40 feet or more.

AN INTRIGUING ISLAND BED

*To brighten a strategic corner of your yard, plant a freestanding,
kidney-shaped island bed of sun-loving perennials.*

Creating an island bed is an easy, fun project, especially for beginning perennial gardeners. Unlike a traditional perennial border set against a hedge or wall, an island bed is surrounded by open space. The gently curving outline of an island bed fits gracefully into the landscape. It's especially satisfying to stroll leisurely around a well-designed perennial island bed, noticing and enjoying the changing view of flowers and foliage from each point.

The Intriguing Island Bed is designed to be placed near a driveway, walkway, or patio, close enough so you can enjoy the cool lavender and blue flowers. Because you would view this bed mostly from one side, it has the tallest flowers planted at the "back" – the side farthest from the walkway, patio, or other main vantage point.

This garden has plenty of color and interest all season long, beginning with spring-blooming bulbs including daffodils and Siberian squill. The tall blue flower spikes of Russian sage, the tallest plant in the garden, appear in summer and last for more than one month. Fall brings more lovely blossoms of Frikart's aster, and the dried seedheads of 'Autumn Joy' sedum look beautiful through the winter.

▲ **As spring turns** to summer in this island bed, daffodils and other bulbs fade back, hidden by the fresh foliage of other perennials. The blue flowers of Siberian iris and purple-leaved ajuga hint at the floral display to come.

The Planting Plan. It's a good idea to use an edging of plastic, metal, or fiberglass to keep lawngrass from creeping into the garden. Remove the fading flowers on rose verbena, Endress cranesbill, 'Happy Returns' daylily, and Frikart's aster to encourage a long bloom period. Frikart's aster may droop when in bloom and can look lovely cascading over the nearby silvermound artemisia. But if you prefer it upright, pinch the shoots back in spring to make the plant grow lower and bushier. If the silvermound artemisia tends to flop open from the center, divide it and avoid fertilizing it.

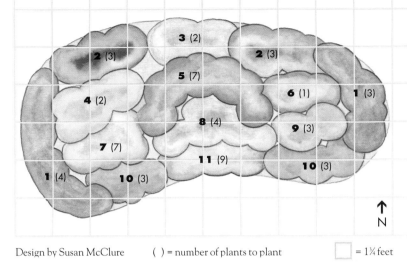

Design by Susan McClure   ( ) = number of plants to plant   ☐ = 1¼ feet

1 Rose verbena (*Verbena canadensis*)

2 'Caesar's Brother' Siberian iris (*Iris sibirica* 'Caesar's Brother')

3 'Mary Ann' daylily (*Hemerocallis* 'Mary Ann') or other tall pink-flowered daylily with daffodils (*Narcissus* spp.)

4 Russian sage (*Perovskia atriplicifolia*)

5 'Autumn Joy' sedum (*Sedum* 'Autumn Joy')

6 'Palest Yellow' daylily (*H.* 'Palest Yellow') or other tall pale daylily with daffodils

7 'Happy Returns' daylily (*H.* 'Happy Returns') with daffodils

8 'A.T. Johnson' Endress cranesbill (*Geranium endressii* 'A.T. Johnson') with daffodils

9 Frikart's aster (*Aster* × *frikartii*)

10 'Nana' silvermound artemisia (*Artemisia schmidtiana* 'Nana')

11 Purple-leaved ajuga (*Ajuga reptans* 'Atropurpurea') with white Siberian squill (*Scilla siberica*)

▲ **In midsummer,** flowers of pink Endress cranesbill and rose verbena may linger on, while a medley of daylilies joins the tall blue spikes of Russian sage. Lavender-blue Frikart's aster adds to the summer show. Pink flowers may start to appear on 'Autumn Joy' sedum.

REARRANGING THE VIEWS If you want to plant the Intriguing Island Bed at a site where you'll view it from all sides, you'll need to reposition the plants so the high point will be in the center of the island. Russian sage is the tallest perennial in this design, so plant it in the center of the bed. Place the medium-height Frikart's aster and 'Autumn Joy' sedum along the boundary of the bed instead of Siberian iris, which will occupy the spot where the Russian sage would have been. The garden remains neatly edged with low silvermound artemisia and purple-leaved ajuga across the front and medium-height rose verbena along the sides. The blue Russian sage and Siberian iris and the tall pink daylilies form a flowering high point in the middle with modest-sized, yellow 'Happy Returns' daylily, pink Endress cranesbill, and lavender Frikart's aster at their feet.

WHERE SHOULD YOUR ISLAND GO? There's almost no limit to the possible sites for a perennial island. You can use island beds to define the boundaries of your yard and to create privacy. They are wonderful for separating parts of your yard that you use for different purposes – such as an outdoor sitting area from your vegetable garden or the children's swing set. They provide a splash of color you can enjoy from your windows, and they make a handsome main attraction when you entertain on the patio. Use island beds near the corner of a patio or along a walk or property line. Stretch island beds under some shade trees or around a cluster of shrubs to make them into a garden feature rather than isolated plants, and to cut down on mowing chores as well.

Sun-drenched areas are ideal for growing the sturdy sun-loving perennials in the Intriguing Island Bed. Island beds around trees or clusters of shrubs are great for perennials that prefer shade. If you plan to create several island beds in your yard, be sure to use a similar color scheme or some of the same plants, so that the beds are tied together by a common thread.

▶ **It's easy** to reposition the plants in the Intriguing Island Bed so that it can be viewed from all sides. Just follow this revised planting plan to make a few changes that place the taller plants in the center of the bed.

( ) = number of plants to plant   ☐ = 1¼ feet

1 Rose verbena (*Verbena canadensis*)

2 'Caesar's Brother' Siberian iris (*Iris sibirica* 'Caesar's Brother')

3 'Mary Ann' daylily (*Hemerocallis* 'Mary Ann') or other tall pink-flowered daylily with daffodils (*Narcissus* spp.)

4 Russian sage (*Perovskia atriplicifolia*)

5 'Autumn Joy' sedum (*Sedum* 'Autumn Joy')

6 'Palest Yellow' daylily (*H*. 'Palest Yellow') or other tall pale daylily with daffodils

7 'Happy Returns' daylily (*H*. 'Happy Returns') with daffodils

8 'A.T. Johnson' Endress cranesbill (*Geranium endressii* 'A.T. Johnson') with daffodils

9 Frikart's aster (*Aster* x *frikartii*)

10 'Nana' silvermound artemisia (*Artemisia schmidtiana* 'Nana')

11 Purple-leaved ajuga (*Ajuga reptans* 'Atropurpurea') with white Siberian squill (*Scilla siberica*)

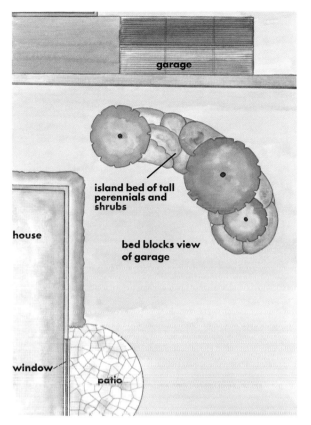

▲ **Plant a sweeping island bed** at the edge of your yard to block an undesirable view.

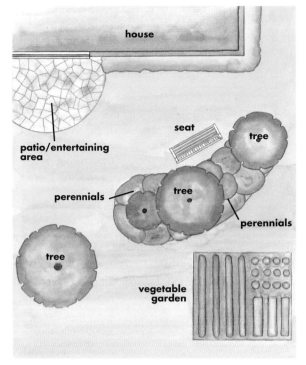

▲ **Separate "outdoor rooms"** with an island bed. For example, you can use a perennial island as the wall between a patio sitting area and a work area that includes your vegetable garden.

TIPS FOR DESIGNING YOUR OWN ISLAND BEDS

Want to try designing an island bed from scratch? It's easy to do. Here are a few simple guidelines to follow:

● For an appealing sense of proportion, make your island beds two to four times longer than they are wide. For example, a 10-foot-wide bed looks well proportioned if it's 20 to 40 feet long.

● Limit the height of the tallest perennials in the bed to about half the width of the bed. For example, if the bed is 6 feet wide, plan on using perennials that top out at about 3 feet tall.

● The organization of the perennials in the bed will vary depending on your main vantage point. If you'll view the island bed equally from all sides, put the tallest perennials in the center of the bed and layer shorter perennials around them. If you see the garden primarily from one direction, put the taller perennials closer to the back and build layers of lower plants in the foreground.

● In an island bed set beneath a tree, let the tallest perennials billow around the base of the tree.

● Cut down on planting time and expense in a large island bed by using perennial groundcovers that spread quickly and are easy to multiply by division. Let low groundcovers, such as moss phlox, cruise across the front and rear of an island bed. Fill the interior of the bed with taller spreading perennials such as daylilies.

● Avoid aggressively spreading perennials like mints (*Mentha* spp.) in island beds. They can quickly overwhelm the other plants.

PROPAGATING PERENNIAL GROUNDCOVERS

Perennial groundcovers are a great choice for an easy-to-plant, low-care island bed. They're especially useful in a shady bed, where you can plant shade-tolerant groundcovers like hostas, ferns, and lilies-of-the-valley to add color and brightness. Whether you're planting in sun or shade, if you propagate your own, you can create beautiful beds for very little money. It's a snap to multiply perennial groundcovers by dividing them, especially groundcovers such as bugleweed, 'Silver King' artemisia, moss phlox, creeping phlox, and others that expand by sending out shoots or roots that creep on or near the soil surface. The best time to divide is during spring and fall, when the plants are emerging from dormancy or about to die back to the ground for winter. For best results, try to divide several months before the perennial usually flowers or before the weather gets severely hot, cold, or dry. (For more on timing, see page 87.)

STARTING A NEW GROUNDCOVER BED STEP-BY-STEP

1 With a sharp trowel or spade, slice through the plant and soil between the main part of the plant and plantlet. Lift the plantlet, keeping as much soil around the roots as you can.

2 Set the plantlets into a sturdy flat or garden cart. It's best to replant them right away. If you can't, wet the roots with a fine spray from the hose, cover the shoots with moist burlap, and move them into a cool, shady spot where they can be kept for a few hours.

3 If you have a large bed to fill with these new plants, gently pull apart the plantlets into single plants, making sure each piece is well supplied with roots and greenery. For smaller spaces, or if you have an abundance of plants, keep the divisions large so they fill out fast.

4 Set the plants in natural-looking groups that wind through the bed, planting them at the same height as they were growing previously. Make sure low-growing perennials are in the foreground and taller perennials are toward the center of the bed. Plant slow-spreading perennials like lady's-mantle 1 foot apart. Space fast spreaders like lily-of-the-valley up to 3 feet apart.

5 Spread a 2-inch layer of organic mulch, like compost, shredded leaves, or fine bark, around the new plants, and water them well. Check them frequently after planting, and keep them moist until they begin to grow vigorously again. Small divisions or plantlets with few roots may need extra coddling.

GROUND-COVERING PERENNIALS

If you've got space to cover, you'll want to try some of these great perennial groundcovers. All of them are easy to divide. You'll find more information about these perennials in Part 3 of this book.

PLANT NAMES	RATE OF SPREAD	RANGE OF HEIGHT
For Sun		
Bugleweeds (*Ajuga* spp.)	Moderate to fast	4"–12"
Daylilies (*Hemerocallis* spp. and cultivars)	Moderate	1'–6'
Kamschatka sedum (*Sedum kamtschaticum*)	Moderate	2"–6"
Lady's-mantle (*Alchemilla mollis*)	Slow	1'
Moss phlox (*Phlox subulata*)	Moderate to fast	4"–8"
Moss verbena (*Verbena tenuisecta*)	Moderate	4"–8"
'Silver King' artemisia (*Artemisia ludoviciana* 'Silver King')	Fast	2'–4'
White stonecrop (*Sedum album*)	Moderate	4"–6"
Yarrows (*Achillea* spp.)	Moderate	1'–4'
For Light Shade		
Allegheny foamflower (*Tiarella cordifolia*)	Moderate	6"–10"
Bigroot cranesbill (*Geranium macrorrhizum*)	Fast	15"–18"
Bugleweeds (*Ajuga* spp.)	Moderate to fast	4"–12"
Creeping phlox (*Phlox stolonifera*)	Moderate	6"–8"
Daylilies (*Hemerocallis* spp.)	Moderate	1'–6'
Epimediums (*Epimedium* spp.)	Moderate	6"–15"
Lady's-mantle (*Alchemilla mollis*)	Slow	1'
Lily-of-the-valley (*Convallaria majalis*)	Fast	6"–8"
Lungworts (*Pulmonaria* spp.)	Moderate	1'–2'
Mints (*Mentha* spp.)	Fast	1'–2½'
Solomon's seals (*Polygonatum* spp.)	Moderate	1'–3'
Violets (*Viola* spp.)	Moderate	1"–12"
Wild gingers (*Asarum* spp.)	Moderate	6"–12"

Kamschatka sedum

Tawny daylily

Solomon's seal

Lungwort

'Rose Queen' epimedium

COLOR THEME GARDENS

Planting a perennial color theme garden is a great way to learn how to create beautiful plant combinations and how to plan a garden that has color and interest all season long.

What would a perennial garden be without color? Colors set the mood of a garden and bring garden scenes to life. With color theme perennial gardens, your options are nearly limitless. You can create a garden around a single color, choose two strongly contrasting colors, or make a rainbow garden of mixed colors. And if you're interested in developing your own original color theme perennial bed, turn to page 26 for detailed directions on creating a color theme garden design.

Planting Plan for a Hot Color Garden. This garden mixes bold, bright flowers in an island bed designed to be viewed from all sides.

1 'Lucifer' crocosmia (*Crocosmia* 'Lucifer') with daffodils (*Narcissus* spp.)

2 Butterfly weed (*Asclepias tuberosa*) with daffodils

3 Woolly yarrow (*Achillea tomentosa*)

4 Pink tickseed (*Coreopsis rosea*)

5 'Early Sunrise' bigflower coreopsis (*Coreopsis grandiflora* 'Early Sunrise') with daffodils

6 'Scarlet Flame' moss phlox (*Phlox subulata* 'Scarlet Flame') or Scarlet Pansy *Viola* x *wittrockiana*

▲ **Summer is hot** in this garden of rich red, brassy pink, and brilliant yellow flowers.

Design by Susan McClure   ( ) = number of plants to plant   ☐ = 1½ feet

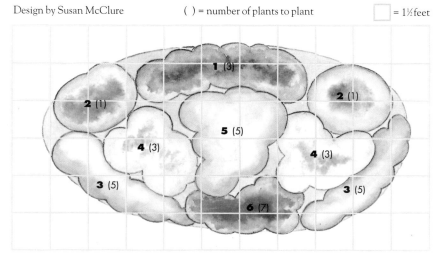

Planting Plan for a Warm Garden.
If you like sunny, vivid colors, you'll enjoy this garden of pure yellow and red flowers. Rose lovers will opt to plant 'Scarlet Meidiland' roses, while peony lovers will choose the spring color and fragrance of peony blossoms. For more information on 'Scarlet Meidiland' roses, see page 35. If peony bloom declines over time, it's a sign that the plants are overcrowded. Lift the clumps in late summer, divide them, and replant. 'Moonbeam' coreopsis will bloom much of the summer and into fall if deadheaded. 'September Ruby' aster will need staking for support.

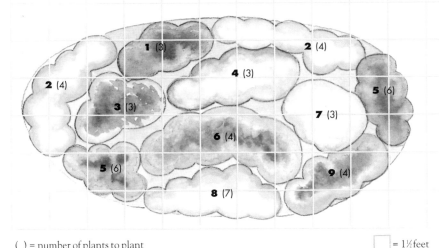

( ) = number of plants to plant   = 1½ feet

1 'September Ruby' New England aster (*Aster novae-angliae* 'September Ruby')

2 'Moonbeam' coreopsis (*Coreopsis verticillata* 'Moonbeam')

3 'Ruby Throat' daylily (*Hemerocallis* 'Ruby Throat') or 'Lucifer' crocosmia (*Crocosmia* 'Lucifer')

4 'Hoffnung' yarrow (*Achillea* 'Hoffnung')

5 'Palace Purple' heuchera (*Heuchera* 'Palace Purple')

6 Red-flowered hybrid peony (*Paeonia* hybrid) or 'Scarlet Meidiland' rose (*Rosa* 'Scarlet Meidiland') with daffodils (*Narcissus* spp.)

7 'Paprika' yarrow (*Achillea* 'Paprika')

8 'Mt. St. Helens' coral bells (*Heuchera x brizoides* 'Mt. St. Helens') with red and yellow tulips (*Tulipa* spp.)

9 'Jenny' New York aster (*Aster novi-belgii* 'Jenny')

▼ **Summer finds this garden** in top form with red and soft yellow yarrows, airy yellow coreopsis blossoms, red roses and daylilies, and delicate coral bells in the foreground.

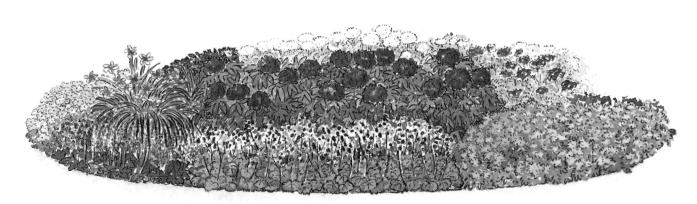

Planting Plan for a Garden with Contrasting Colors. If you're looking for truly eye-catching combinations, try this design featuring blue-, yellow-, and white-flowering perennials and bulbs. The jonquils and daffodils provide early color, and the developing perennials will hide the bulb foliage as it dies back. The compact 'Purple Dome' asters should not need staking. If your garden has very rich soil, the violet sage may tend to flop if not supported. If you choose to plant blue false indigo instead of Siberian iris, plant only four plants.

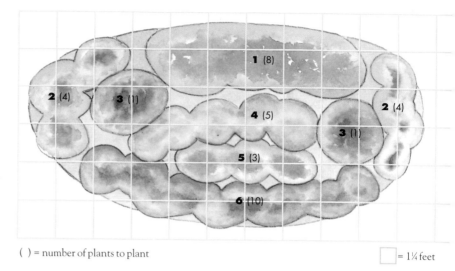

( ) = number of plants to plant   ☐ = 1¼ feet

1 Purple or blue variety of Siberian iris (*Iris sibirica*) or blue false indigo (*Baptisia australis*) with trumpet daffodils (*Narcissus* spp.)

2 'East Friesland' violet sage (*Salvia* × *superba* 'East Friesland')

3 'Hidcote' lavender (*Lavandula angustifolia* 'Hidcote')

4 'Moonbeam' coreopsis (*Coreopsis verticillata* 'Moonbeam')

5 'Purple Dome' New England aster (*Aster novae-angliae* 'Purple Dome')

6 Purple-leaved ajuga (*Ajuga reptans* 'Atropurpurea') with jonquils (*Narcissus jonquilla*)

▼ **In late summer,** purple is the dominant color in this contrasting garden, set off by the clear yellow blossoms of 'Moonbeam' coreopsis.

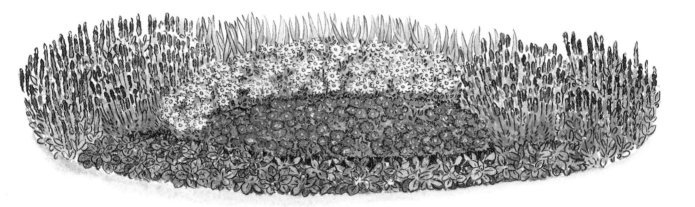

▲ **Early summer** features airy sprays of colewort at the center of the pastel garden. Sea-pinks add cheerful pink in front, flanked by blue and white cranesbills.

Planting Plan for a Pastel Garden. This garden features pink, blue, and white flowers, which always make great companions. Choose a mix of crocus cultivars that reflect this color theme. 'Album' blood-red cranesbill is a surprising white-flowered cultivar of this normally pink- or red-flowering perennial. Keep in mind that balloon flowers are slow to emerge in spring. Clip off fading blooms from balloon flowers and Stokes' asters to extend their bloom season into fall.

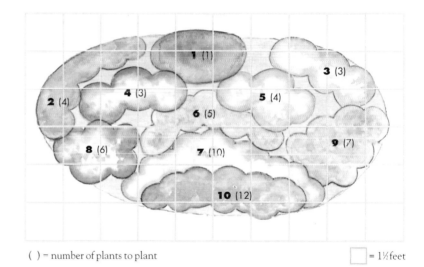

( ) = number of plants to plant   ☐ = 1½ feet

1 Colewort (*Crambe cordifolia*)

2 Blue-flowered balloon flower (*Platycodon grandiflorus*) with grape hyacinths (*Muscari* spp.)

3 White-flowered balloon flower with grape hyacinths

4 'Appleblossom' yarrow (*Achillea* 'Appleblossom')

5 'Margarete' Japanese anemone (*Anemone* x *hybrida* 'Margarete')

6 Blue-flowered Stokes' aster (*Stokesia laevis*)

7 White-flowered Stokes' aster

8 'Album' blood-red cranesbill (*Geranium sanguineum* 'Album')

9 'Johnson's Blue' cranesbill (*Geranium* 'Johnson's Blue')

10 Sea-pink (*Armeria maritima*) with crocuses (*Crocus* spp.)

DEVELOPING YOUR OWN COLOR THEME To get ideas for color theme gardens, look at photographs of perennial gardens in books and magazines. Visit botanical gardens or the display gardens at a local nursery. You might even get ideas for color combinations from a pretty wallpaper or fabric pattern – just let your imagination go!

Draw your own color wheel like this one to help plan a color theme garden. To find pairs of exciting contrasting colors, lay a ruler directly across the wheel. The two colors that the ruler touches, like yellow and violet, are contrasting. Adjacent colors, like blue and blue-green, are harmonious and calming.

If you like bold, bright gardens, choose flowers with contrasting colors such as violet and yellow, blue and orange, or red and green. For a more restful garden, mix colors that are close, such as yellow and orange or blue and violet.

Try setting cool colors in front of a warm-colored background, such as blue flowers in front of red flowers. The contrast will make the cool colors more noticeable. Warm colors stand out even right at the back of the yard. To soften the warm colors, use pastels such as lemon yellow, apricot orange, or pink, and blend them with cooler colors.

When you create a color theme garden, you can maintain the same colors throughout the growing season or let them change. For instance, a warm color garden could feature sunny yellows and whites in spring, change to many colors in early summer, move to golds and violets in late summer, and then to fall crimsons and bronze.

MAKE A COLOR VALUE FINDER A color value finder is a homemade collection of color samples. You can use it to keep track of the true colors of the perennials that you come across in gardens or at nurseries. This will help you when you select perennials for a color theme garden.

To make a color value finder, collect paint chips (you can get these at any paint store) that show clear primary colors as well as more complex colors. You'll want to include yellow, yellow-green, green, blue-green, blue, blue-violet, violet, red-violet, red, orange-red, orange, and yellow-orange. The paint chips will also show the pastel tints and darker shades of these colors. Each color on a chip is identified by a name or number. (The names may be fanciful, like "Free Spirit" or "Bianca," rather than descriptive of the color, but they'll still serve your purpose here.)

Staple or glue each chip on a separate piece of paper in a small notebook. Take the notebook along with you when you shop or visit a botanical garden. When you see a perennial that appeals to you, match its color to one of the colors on a paint chip in your color value finder. Make a note of the plant name and color.

When you're ready to plan a garden, pull out your color value finder and your notes. By referring to the paint chips, you'll get a true picture of the colors you'll get in your garden and can group plants according to your tastes.

Keep an accurate record of the flower colors of perennials you've admired at gardens and nurseries with a color value finder.

PICKING COLOR THEME PLANTS You'll find lots of variety in the descriptions of flower colors in perennial catalogs and books. One source will call a certain flower scarlet while another calls it bright pink. It's best to confirm the color of a perennial for yourself before you choose it for a garden. (One way to keep records of the true colors of perennials is with a color value finder like the one described on the opposite page.)

When you're designing a color theme garden, you'll want to start with two main colors. You may pick two of your favorite colors, or you may decide that your color theme should pick up the colors of the interior of your home or of your exterior shutters or walks.

The best combinations often come from pure colors – such as blue, red, orange, violet or yellow. But flowers with different undertones – such as salmon-pink and lavender pink – usually clash. You can refer to the color wheel on the opposite page to learn more about the relationships between colors.

Also consider leaf color – dark green, purple, silver, chartreuse, gold, or even black – that can serve as a third accent color or one of the two main colors. One easy way to maintain a unified color theme over several seasons is to include a few long-blooming plants such as coreopsis or black-eyed Susans.

REFINING A COLOR THEME GARDEN You can refine a color theme garden even after it's planted and growing. You may decide that the colors aren't balanced. Perhaps there's too much violet in one half of the garden and hardly any in the other. Or you may decide you want yellow as an accent of color that repeats throughout the design. After all, experimenting with color is what a color theme garden is all about.

If you do decide to change a garden, make notes about which plants you want to move or divide and where you'll move them to. Then wait until the plants finish blooming, and dig them up and replant them. Pamper them a bit until they reestablish themselves, and then wait to see how your new perennial color picture turns out!

SKETCHING A GARDEN DESIGN Using catalogs, books, and your color value finder with notes on perennial colors, select perennials with appropriate flower colors.

1 Use a pencil to sketch your garden site to scale on a piece of graph paper. The scale of ¼ inch to 1 foot should work for most small or moderate-size gardens.

2 Draw circles and ovals in the garden to represent each type of perennial. Put the tallest perennial toward the rear of the garden. Then fill in a front edging of low growing perennials. Add in more perennials from side to side, using a balanced blend of colors on either side. You can repeat clusters of the same plant or use different plants that have the same colors.

3 Put tracing paper over your garden plan, and use markers or colored pencils to fill in the flower colors of the plants that will bloom in spring. Then take another piece of tracing paper and color in the summer bloomers, and a third for the fall bloomers. You may need to change some of your plant choices to ensure that the colors are nicely coordinated through the seasons.

A SERENE
SHADE GARDEN

*With easy-care perennials that love shade, you can turn a stark area
under trees into a beautiful, colorful garden retreat.*

Anemones, foamflowers, astilbes, goat's beard, bleeding hearts, and lily-of-the-valley all thrive in light shade. In the Serene Shade Garden, you'll find all of these lovely flowers, along with the handsome foliage of variegated Solomon's seal and Japanese painted fern.

Foliage texture and form also play an important role: divided leaves of anemones, toothed foamflower leaves, upright swordlike leaves of lily-of-the-valley, arching stems of Solomon's seal, heart-shaped epimedium foliage, and the bold, dark green leaves of black snakeroot. Together, they create a garden that lures you closer to investigate its subtle beauty. Shafts of light filtering through the tree branches overhead and the rustling of the leaves will add even more pleasure to your visit to the Serene Shade Garden.

▶ **Soft pastels** fill a woodland garden in spring. Spring-blooming shade perennials include epimedium, fragrant wild blue phlox, delicate white spikes of Allegheny foamflower, bell-shaped Solomon's seal, and lily-of-the-valley blossoms.

The Planting Plan. This design features a pebbled path that loops around two shade trees, and a bench for sitting and enjoying the garden. The narrow planting beds are extra-easy to tend. Watch for slugs on the hostas, and keep the soil moist for top performance from astilbes, Solomon's seal, and Allegheny foamflower.

1 'Margarete' Japanese anemone
(*Anemone* x *hybrida* 'Margarete')

2 'Superba' fall astilbe
(*Astilbe taquetu* 'Superba')

3 Wild blue phlox (*Phlox divaricata*)

4 Epimedium (*Epimedium* spp.)

5 Wild bleeding heart
(*Dicentra eximia*)

6 Black snakeroot
(*Cimicifuga racemosa*)

7 'Rheinland' astilbe
(*Astilbe* x *arendsii* 'Rheinland')

8 Japanese painted fern
(*Athyrium goeringianum* 'Pictum')

9 Lily-of-the-valley
(*Convallaria majalis*)

10 Solomon's seal
(*Polygonatum biflorum*)

11 'Elegans' Siebold's hosta
(*Hosta sieboldiana* 'Elegans')

12 Goat's beard (*Aruncus dioicus*)

13 Allegheny foamflower
(*Tiarella cordifolia*)

14 'Ginko Craig' hosta
(*Hosta* 'Ginko Craig')

15 'Whirlwind' Japanese anemone

16 Variegated Solomon's seal
(*Polygonatum odoratum* 'Variegatum')

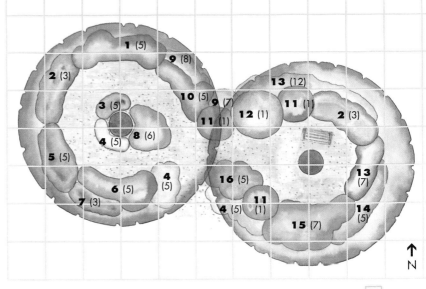

Design by Robin A. Siktberg   ( ) = number of plants to plant   ☐ = 2¾ feet

N ↑

▶ **Fall brings red and yellow** to the trees that shelter the Serene Shade Garden. In the garden itself, the foliage of many perennials also turns a lovely yellow, and clouds of white anemone flowers emerge.

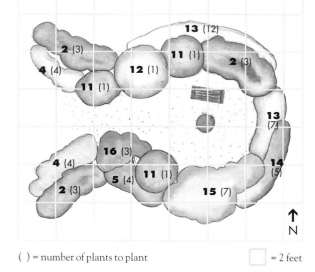

( ) = number of plants to plant   ☐ = 2 feet

CREATING YOUR OWN SHADE Shade trees aren't an absolute requirement for creating a shade garden. You can plant a lovely shade garden under an arbor topped with lath or wooden beams. In fact, your plants may be happiest growing under an arbor, where they'll have light shade, but no tree roots competing for moisture and nutrients.

An arbor can be rustic or ornate, whatever matches your home and landscape. You can make a simple arbor by erecting two rows of 4 × 4 wooden posts and topping them with lath. Plant vines such as clematis, trumpet creeper (*Campsis radicans*), hardy kiwi (*Actinidia arguta*), or silver lace vine (*Polygonum aubertii*) by the posts; the vines will climb them and fill in overhead.

To adapt the Serene Shade Garden for planting under an arbor, choose a selection of the plants used, and group them in pleasing combinations. Choose the smaller perennials for best results – goat's beard, 'Elegans' hosta, and black snakeroot are so large that they would overwhelm the space under an arbor. Leave an open area in the center for a piece of garden sculpture or a bench.

A GARDEN FOR A SINGLE TREE If you only have a single shade tree in your yard, adapt the plan for the Serene Shade Garden by planting half of the garden. Create an inviting entrance that guides visitors to the garden with curved beds of epimedium backed by astilbes. (Refer to page 29 for the list of plants.)

▶ **A wooden arbor** covered by vines like trumpet creeper, clematis, and hardy kiwi creates a pretty setting for enjoying shade-loving perennials.

SCREENS FOR SHADE AND PRIVACY A fence or hedge that runs from east to west or from northwest to southeast will cast shade during a good portion of the day. Plant a shady perennial garden next to it, and you'll create a peaceful outdoor retreat where you can relax on weekends, visit with friends, or just sit and enjoy the flowers. A screen can divide different parts of your landscape, separating a quiet reading corner from your entertaining patio, and it can also make a nice backdrop for a garden.

Living screens include hedges, shrubs, and ornamental grasses. You can also screen areas with fences, walls, and trellises. Here are some points to consider when choosing a screen.

Evergreens. Plant a staggered double line of conifers such as pines, spruces, or hemlocks. In time, they will mature to form a solid wall of greenery. For immediate privacy, you'll need to start with 5- or 6-foot-tall trees. Your privacy will become more complete as the trees grow, even blocking views from your neighbor's second-story windows.

Hedges. If you have time to let a hedge develop, it can be a lovely and relatively inexpensive alternative to fencing. A hedge of needle-leaved evergreens will give you year-round screening and foliage interest. Some broad-leaved evergreens, such as rhododendrons, also bear flowers. Deciduous shrubs, which hold their leaves only through the growing season, may be suitable if you only need privacy for fair-weather outdoor forays. Deciduous shrubs can be more interesting than evergreens, providing a progression of flowers, fruit, and fall color.

Shrub Clusters. A cluster of three or five shrubs can provide a perfect screen for a small open area. Shrub clusters are less expensive than hedges and can be more relaxed and natural looking – and they're also a lot less work.

Fences. Fences are a good choice when you want instant shade and privacy. A 4-foot-tall fence makes a nice screen. In a low-lying yard, you may need a taller fence. Fences do require some maintenance (especially wooden ones). Check municipal or neighborhood regulations about fences before you finalize your plans.

Walls. To create the impression of privacy without a tall fence, try building a low stone or brick wall, and create a garden beside it that includes some tall plants. For example, you could combine perennials with tall ornamental grasses like maiden grasses (*Miscanthus* spp.), or plant shrubs and small ornamental trees like crabapples, dogwoods, redbuds, or viburnums.

Trellises. A tightly woven lattice lets in little of the outside world; an open lattice serves mostly as a symbolic garden wall. To make a more effective screen, plant vines to climb the lattice, and then add perennials in front.

▲ **A mature evergreen hedge** creates a natural wall that screens noise and traffic and is a great backdrop for warm-colored perennials.

▲**Low-growing branches** on large shade trees can block so much light that it's hard to grow anything beneath them (*left*). Have an arborist remove a few limbs to let in light and create a good garden site (*right*).

5 TRICKS TO BRING LIGHT TO YOUR SHADY SITE

Lots of lovely plants bloom in partial shade. But there just aren't many perennials that will bloom in deep shade. So if your yard seems dominated by dark, gloomy areas, try some of the following techniques to let in more light. Then you'll have a greater variety of shade-tolerant flowers to choose from when creating easy-care shade gardens.

Thin Out Undergrowth. If your shady area is tangled with young saplings and shrubs, very little light will reach the perennials below. Before preparing the garden bed in an overgrown area like this, cut back some of the excess brush.

Limb Up Trees. Remove lower limbs on shade trees so that sunlight will reach the area underneath them in the morning and late afternoon. (Another benefit is that you won't run into the branches as you mow the lawn.) It's smart to call a professional arborist for this type of job.

Thin Out Tree Limbs. To let light through thickly branched shade trees, consider having a professional arborist thin branches. Direct arborist crews to cut out small and medium-sized branches to reduce foliage density. They can also remove any main limbs that arise directly under another branch or are crossing, rubbing, or diseased. A word of advice: NEVER ask an arborist to top a tree or cut limbs back partway. This damages the tree, and the resulting bushy regrowth will block all light to the ground besides.

Start Smart. Some trees, such as honey locusts and birches, have naturally open branching or fine leaves that allow some sun through without any extra pruning. If you are starting a shade garden from scratch, these are great trees to plant. Other deciduous trees, even those with heavy canopies, allow enough light through in spring before the tree leaves open to support the growth of spring-blooming bulbs. Most evergreen trees, however, cast heavy shade year-round.

Maximize Sunlight. Make the most of sunlight by planting where the sun shines the longest. Unless blocked by shadows, the sun touches the southern side of a grove of trees all day. It reaches the eastern side in the morning and the western side in the afternoon. The northern side of the grove will be in shadow most of the day and will have the least amount of sun.

6 WAYS TO MAKE DARK SPOTS SEEM BRIGHTER

Sometimes there's just no easy way to get more sun to a site – for example, when a solid building is what's blocking the sun. Here are some simple suggestions that will make a shady spot seem brighter.

Emphasize Light-Colored Flowers. Select plants with bright white or light pastel flowers that reflect light and stand out in shadows. For maximum impact, choose perennials with large, open-faced flowers, such as anemones, or dense clusters of small flowers, such as astilbes. And don't turn your nose up at mixing in shade-tolerant annuals like white-flowered impatiens.

Dabble in Variegated Foliage. Many of the nicest hostas have foliage edged or marked with white or cream. Variegated Solomon's seal also gives dark areas the appearance of dappled sunlight. Bright flowers come and go through the seasons, but variegated foliage remains bright spring, summer, and fall.

▲ **To transform a dreary corner,** plant a light-colored planter like this urn with colorful, shade-tolerant impatiens.

◀ **Choose interesting foliage** to light up shady plantings such as variegated Solomon's seal and hostas.

Brighten the Scene with Light-Colored Bark. Consider growing trees such as beeches or birches that have light-colored bark. Beeches (*Fagus* spp.) have tight, smooth silver bark. Easy-care monarch birch (*Betula maximowicziana*) has cinnamon-colored bark that brightens to pale gray with maturity.

Display Plants in Bright Pots. Highlight your shade garden with flowering or foliage plants in light-colored pots. Choose from cement, cast stone, or carved stone planters in white or light gray. Bring ceramic or stoneware pots inside when temperatures drop below freezing to prevent cracking.

Think White for Furniture and Structures. Bright white lawn furniture will glow in a shady garden sitting area. Light-colored or painted wood on nearby trellises and arbors will do the same.

Pave the Path with White Stones. A path of light-colored stones looks cool and inviting heading into a shady spot, while a dark gravel path just seems to disappear in shadows.

A ROMANTIC PERENNIAL, HERB, AND ROSE GARDEN

You can create a beautiful, fragrant garden with plants to use in cooking and crafts by combining easy-care perennials, roses, and herbs.

This garden features a rainbow carpet of aromatic gold and silver oregano, thyme, lavender, and sage. It also includes great perennials for cutting, drying, and wreath making, such as yarrow, lady's-mantle, purple coneflowers, globe thistle, and sea holly. Most of these flowers will bloom from summer into fall if you deadhead the old flowers regularly. The semiformal half-moon bed is perfect for planting beside a deck or patio, where it will add a romantic and fragrant atmosphere when you sit outside to enjoy some time with special friends.

The Romantic Perennial, Herb, and Rose Garden features high-powered perennials that need full sun, at least 6 hours a day. The herbs and everlastings (flowers that are perfect for drying) also insist on well-drained, sandy soil. If you have clay soil, it's a good idea to build raised beds and amend the soil with lots of organic matter before planting these plants. You'll also find that the silver-leaved plants in this garden, such as silver thyme and alpine sea holly, will benefit from a mulch of coarse sand instead of organic matter.

▼ **Summer contrasts** in this garden include golden yarrow and blue-flowered globe thistle and sea holly. Roses and purple coneflowers add to the show.

The Planting Plan. Like spokes on a wagon wheel, brick dividers separate the garden into four wedges. The wedges adjacent to the patio feature gold and scarlet plants. The other sections provide cool contrast with silver foliage and blue or purple flowers.

1 Lavender
(*Lavandula angustifolia*)

2 Silver thyme
(*Thymus argenteus*)

3 Purple coneflower
(*Echinacea purpurea*)

4 Garden sage
(*Salvia officinalis*)

5 'Taplow Blue' globe
thistle (*Echinops ritro*
'Taplow Blue')

6 Alpine sea holly
(*Eryngium alpinum*)

7 Silvermound artemisia
(*Artemisia schmidtiana*
'Nana')

8 Lady's-mantle
(*Alchemilla mollis*)

9 Golden oregano
(*Origanum vulgare*
'Aureum' or
'Dr. Ietswaart')

10 'Scarlet Meidiland'
rose (*Rosa* 'Scarlet
Meidiland')

11 'Coronation Gold'
yarrow (*Achillea*
'Coronation Gold')

12 Golden sage (*Salvia
officinalis* 'Aurea')
with Siberian squill
(*Scilla siberica*)

13 Golden lemon thyme
(*Thymus* × *citriodorus*
'Aureus')

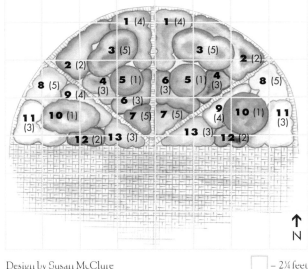

Design by Susan McClure
( ) = number of plants to plant

☐ = 2¼ feet

EASY-CARE ROSES, HERBS, AND EVERLASTINGS This garden design features some special perennial herbs and everlasting flowers that aren't included in Part 3 of this book. But like the other easy-care perennials described there, these grow with no fuss as long as they have well-drained soil and full sun.

Alpine sea holly bears small steel-blue flowers surrounded by purple-blue bracts (modified leaves). Zones 3 to 8.

Golden lemon thyme, a low-grower with gold-marked foliage, has a lovely lemon scent. Zones 5 to 9.

Golden oregano, a creeping golden-leaved oregano, forms a handsome groundcover. Zones 4 to 9.

Golden sage has gold-variegated foliage and will tolerate drought. Zones 3 to 9.

'Scarlet Meidiland' rose is a disease-resistant landscape rose with arching branches up to 3 feet tall. Cut the flower in bud to dry for potpourri or wreaths. Because roses need more nourishment than herbs, provide extra compost, and fertilize and water regularly. Zones 4 to 8.

Silver thyme, a creeping blue-flowered thyme, has gray and cream variegation in its leaves. Zones 5 to 9.

'Taplow Blue' globe thistle features globe-shaped blue flowers that reach 2½ feet tall. The plants have spiny thistlelike leaves. Zones 3 to 8.

RAISING THE GARDEN If you have an elevated deck or patio, you'll enjoy this garden more if you raise it up to the same level. You can raise the bed by building a low semicircular retaining wall, and filling the enclosed area with soil and compost.

If you don't want to fuss with laying brick to make the retaining wall and dividers for this garden, try using rot-resistant wood such as locust. If you use wooden timbers, you'll need to alter the shape of the garden. It will become a half-octagon instead of a circle.

GROWING ANNUAL EVERLASTINGS Some of the most popular and striking everlasting flowers are annuals like strawflowers rather than perennials. As long as your garden gets plenty of sun, you can substitute annual everlastings for the perennials in this garden. Keep in mind that annual everlastings need extra moisture and very fertile soil for best growth.

One of the prettiest annual everlastings is 'Pink Flamingo' cockscomb (*Celosia cristata* 'Pink Flamingo'), with feathery flower plumes that are lavender or pink at

▲ **Make a beautiful addition** to a raised deck by planting a raised bed of roses, perennials, and herbs alongside it.

◀ **Use annuals** like globe amaranth to add vibrant color to dried perennial arrangements. Grow them in full sun and very fertile soil for the best flowers.

the base fading to white at the tip. Another popular annual for dried flower crafts is globe amaranth (*Gomphrena globosa*). Its nickel-size, globelike flowers can be pink, violet, white, red, or orange.

Strawflowers (*Helichrysum bracteatum*) are a standard for dried arrangements. Their vivid daisylike flowers have petals that feel as dry as straw. They come in shades of pink, red, yellow, and white. Statice (*Limonium sinuatum*) has upright spikes of papery flowers in bright blue, pink, purple, yellow, or white.

EASY-CARE ROSES Roses are wonderful companions for perennials and herbs – just be sure you choose roses that are easy to care for! You can start with old-fashioned roses such as fragrant French rose (*Rosa gallica*) and Damask rose (*R. damascena*). These roses are hardy and resistant to diseases, but they bloom primarily in early summer. Even better are newer hybrid shrub roses that bloom repeatedly through summer and fall. Here are some of the best:

'The Fairy' bears many small pink flowers in summer and fall, and forms a neat mound about 3 feet tall and wide. Zones 5 to 9.

Meidiland roses are hybrid spreading roses that bloom heavily in late spring, and then rebloom in summer

and fall. White 'Alba Meidiland' grows as a groundcover to 30 inches tall. 'Scarlet Meidiland' reaches 3 feet tall and spreads up to 6 feet wide. Zones 4 to 8.

Rugosa rose (*R. rugosa*) is tough, disease-resistant, and salt-tolerant. It grows into a large shrub, 4 to 6 feet tall, with pink, white, or red flowers in late spring and summer. Zones 2 to 9.

'Sea Foam' has pink buds and fragrant white flowers in early summer, and reblooms almost continuously for the rest of the growing season. It grows to 3 feet tall and can spread up to 8 feet wide. Zones 4 to 9.

To get the best from easy-care roses, plant them in rich and moist but well-drained soil in full sun. Fertilize in spring and summer with a balanced organic fertilizer. Prune off dead, damaged, or diseased branches whenever you find them. Water as needed to keep the soil evenly moist.

You can cut rosebuds for drying when they are colored but still closed. They make a wonderful addition to potpourri. Some roses produce tart, berrylike rose hips that are rich in vitamin C and make a good ingredient in herb teas. Harvest rose hips when they are bright red, dry them for several weeks, and then grind or crush them for teas.

DRYING FLOWERS AND HERBS To enjoy the beauty and color of your perennial, herb, and rose garden year-round, plan on cutting and drying some of its bounty of flowers and colorful foliage. Harvest flowers for drying when they are young, fresh, and showing perfect color. A great time to harvest is midmorning, after dew has dried off the petals. Herbs and everlasting flowers usually dry well in a warm, dark, well-ventilated room or shed, and can be stored in a firm-sided plastic storage box. Other flowers need to be covered with a drying agent like silica gel for best results.

Upright Drying. Dry large or full flowers like yarrow upright so they maintain their open shape. Gather small bunches of stems and set them upright in dry vases or put individual stems in a drying rack. To make your own drying rack, cut holes in the sides of a cardboard box and set a wire mesh screen on top. Stick stems of perennial flowers through the screen to dry upright.

After the flower petals dry, lay the stems on a table in front of an air conditioner or in a well-ventilated attic to finish drying.

Dangle Drying. Plants with narrow stems like lavender dry well if you bundle them and hang them in a well-ventilated room or attic (their colors may stay brighter if you keep them in a dark spot).

Harvest flower stems and leafy sprigs. Make sure each piece you harvest has at least 4 inches of stem. Hang the stems to dry in bundles of up to ½ inch thick, and hold each bundle together with a twist tie. If humidity is high, make the bundles smaller. Thick-stemmed flowers such as astilbes or asters should be left to dry individually. Dangle the bundles or individual stems from a drying rack or coat hanger and leave them to dry.

Drying with Silica Gel. Silica gel works well for drying thick succulent flowers like peonies and rosebuds. Do not treat edible flowers or herbs you want to use for cooking with silica gel.

Harvest flower buds and newly opened flowers. Remove the stems or strip off the leaves. Put a 1-inch layer of silica gel in the bottom of a plastic container that has an airtight lid. Set individual flowers in it, placing them so they don't touch.

Work additional silica gel around the petals, then cover the flowers completely. Layer in more flowers and silica gel until the container is full and seal it. Leave the flowers stored in the silica gel until you're ready to use them.

▶ **Plants dry** well hanging in a well-ventilated room. Keeping them in a dark place may help to preserve their colors.

MAKING A SIMPLE WREATH

Once you have a collection of dried flowers and herbs, don't let them sit in boxes. You can easily turn them into a lovely wreath to hang on your kitchen door or living room wall. It will lift your spirits and remind you on chilly winter days that another gardening season is just a few short months away.

You will need:

- Dried flowers, petals, and leaves; dried herbs
- A straw or grass wreath base
- Clear, quick-setting glue or a hot glue gun
- 8-inch length of medium-gauge florist's wire
- Ribbon

1 Gather your materials on a table or work area. Choose ribbon that complements the colors of the dried flowers and herbs.

2 Spread a thick layer of glue on a small area of the wreath base. Make sure the glue spreads into the nooks and crannies of the wreath surface.

3 Press petals and leaves firmly onto the glue. Then spread glue on another section of the wreath and press on more dried material. Repeat until the sides and top surface of the wreath are covered.

4 Gather a bunch of dried herbs and flowers and cut the stems short. Wrap the piece of wire around the stems, then tie the ribbon around the bunch and make a bow. Push the ends of the wire into the wreath base to fasten the bunch in place.

▶ **An herb and everlasting wreath** makes a beautiful and fragrant keepsake of your perennial, herb, and rose garden.

A COLONIAL COTTAGE GARDEN

*Cottage gardens have been around since the Middle Ages,
but they're still the freshest, most fun gardening style around.*

In a cottage garden, anything goes. Originally, gardeners grew vegetables, herbs, flowers, and even fruit trees together in their cottage gardens. By Victorian times, the cottage garden had become a fragrant, colorful mix of heirloom flowers and prized varieties.

A cottage garden is a very informal garden. Plants spread and mingle, creating a rich mix of colors and textures. The natural combinations are beautiful, but to get the most from your garden, you'll need to enforce a little organization. This design mixes cottage garden plants with a colonial garden layout. The design holds the plants firmly in check with a picket fence and brick or stone pathways that divide the garden into four beds. The pathways between beds and stepping-stones in the beds offer easy access whenever you need to plunge in and cut back or divide a spreading perennial that threatens to swamp its neighbors. They also let you wander in all parts of the garden, inviting you to admire its beauty and fragrance up close or to cut a bouquet of fresh flowers.

▼ **Lavender and 'Heritage' roses** fill the Colonial Cottage Garden with color and fragrance in early summer. Bugleweed, Siberian iris, and peonies also add their lovely flowers to this charming setting.

The Planting Plan. The garden starts with a framework of roses, hydrangeas, and easy-care perennials, including lavender, daylilies, anemones, violets, bugleweed, and spring bulbs. You give the design your unique style by filling in the framework with your choices of plants from "Perennials for Your Sunny Cottage Garden." You'll need to make your own decisions regarding the number of each type to plant. See "How Many Perennials Should You Buy?" on page 79 for guidance. When you plant these beds, put the shortest plants next to the paths, then place other plants by height, building to the showstopper perennials in the center.

Design by Susan McClure   ☐ = 3¼ feet   ↑ N

1 'Heritage' rose
   (*Rosa* 'Heritage')

2 Japanese anemone
   (*Anemone* × *hybrida*)

3 'Forever Pink' bigleaf
   hydrangea (*Hydrangea
   macrophylla* 'Forever Pink')

4 Showstopper plants

5 Edging plants

6 Lavender (*Lavandula
   angustifolia*)

7 Daylilies (*Hemerocallis*
   spp.) with daffodils
   (*Narcissus* spp.)

8 'Hooks' juniper
   (*Juniperus chinensis*
   'Hooks')

9 Medium-height plants

10 Siberian iris
   (*Iris sibirica*)

11 Labrador violet
   (*Viola labradorica*)
   with *Tulipa tarda* and
   bugleweed (*Ajuga* spp.)

PERENNIALS FOR YOUR SUNNY COTTAGE GARDEN

The lists below separate easy-care perennials and bulbs into categories so it's easy to see where they can fit into the Colonial Cottage Garden. To give your garden a more restful, designed look, plant clumps of three or more of each plant together and repeat plantings of the same plant in two or more beds. You'll find more information about how to grow each of the plants in Part 3 of this book.

Edging Plants

Crocuses (*Crocus* spp.)

Grape hyacinths (*Muscari* spp.)

Grecian windflower (*Anemone
   blanda*)

Jonquil (*Narcissus jonquilla*)

Lady's-mantle (*Alchemilla mollis*)

'Nana' silvermound artemisia
   (*Artemisia schmidtiana* 'Nana')

Pasque flower (*Anemone pulsatilla*)

Rose verbena (*Verbena canadensis*)

Sea-pink (*Armeria maritima*)

Siberian squill (*Scilla siberica*)

Tulips (*Tulipa greigii*)

Winter aconite (*Eranthis hyemalis*)

Woolly yarrow (*Achillea tomentosa*)

Medium-Height Plants

Butterfly weed (*Asclepias tuberosa*)

Coral bells (*Heuchera sanguinea*)

Daffodils (*Narcissus* spp.)

'East Friesland' violet sage
   (*Salvia* × *superba* 'East Friesland')

'Goldsturm' black-eyed Susan
   (*Rudbeckia fulgida* 'Goldsturm')

Hardy geraniums (*Geranium* spp.)

'Jean Davis' or 'Munstead' lavender
   (*Lavandula angustifolia* 'Jean
   Davis' or 'Munstead')

Peony (*Paeonia officinalis*)

Pincushion flower
   (*Scabiosa caucasica*)

Snowdrop anemone
   (*Anemone sylvestris*)

Stokes' aster (*Stokesia laevis*)

Showstopper Plants

Balloon flower (*Platycodon
   grandiflorus*)

Baptisia (*Baptisia australis*)

Coreopsis (*Coreopsis* spp.)

Crocosmias (*Crocosmia* hybrids)

Daylilies (*Hemerocallis* spp.)

Early phlox (*Phlox maculata*)

Purple coneflower (*Echinacea
   purpurea*)

Siberian iris (*Iris sibirica*)

▶ **In an informal cottage garden,** perennials cheerfully mix and mingle. There's no limit to the combinations of colors and textures you can create.

PERSONALIZING THE GARDEN In your cottage garden, you can grow cherished passalong plants from your grandmother's garden, a mix of flowers and herbs, old-fashioned flowers, the latest varieties – or all of the above. A cottage garden is *your* garden in the truest sense of the word: It can be whatever you want to make it. You should feel free to add personal favorite plants, even if they're not in the lists on the preceding page; just place them according to their height.

For a truly cheerful cottage garden look, be sure to include plenty of spring-flowering bulbs between clumps of perennials. Mixing perennials and bulbs has two big pluses. First, the early-blooming bulbs add color in spring, when your perennials are just getting started. Then, when the bulb show ends, the perennial foliage and flowers hide the bulb foliage as it ages and yellows.

Cottage gardens traditionally include old-fashioned flowers such as honeysuckle, sweet peas, columbines (*Aquilegia* spp.), foxgloves, bearded iris, poppies, pansies, and pinks. These plants may not meet an easy-care standard because they need special treatment or are prone to pest problems. However, you may still want to include some of them in your garden to lend it a distinct cottage garden air.

Here are some hints to help you find those special plants that make your cottage garden uniquely your own:
● Seek out a specialty nursery that features old-fashioned or unusual flowers for cutting, fragrance, or drying.
● If your grandparents or other older relatives decide to sell their home, transplant some of their favorite flowers to your garden when they move, and start a family tradition.
● Splurge when spring fever hits. Go ahead and buy that perennial you've been admiring in a mail-order catalog.
● Visit a gardening friend, and ask for a division or cutting of one of her prize plants.
● Pick your favorite era in history – Victorian, Colonial, Elizabethan, or whatever – and grow some of its most popular plants in your garden.

When you've dug plants or taken divisions or cuttings from someone else's garden, check for insect or disease problems before you add the plants to your garden. Take a close look at the tops and undersides of the leaves. Look for insects and insect eggs, or misshapen and discolored leaves. Check the roots and crowns for signs of rot. If you find symptoms, don't keep the plant – put it in a sealed plastic bag and throw it away.

If you're trying out an unfamiliar plant, ask the person who gave it to you how tall it will grow, so you know where to position it in your garden. (You can also find this information in a catalog or perennial encyclopedia.) Check whether it will spread rapidly, and whether it's prone to pest or disease problems. You may decide it's not right for your garden after all. If the plant fits in, however, you'll find that you get twice the enjoyment from it – first, because it's lovely, and second, because you have a special relationship with it.

CREATING A SMALLER GARDEN If you'd like a garden that's smaller than the one shown in the plan, you can easily cut it down to size. Simply plant two sections of the garden on either side of your front door. You can still surround it with a picket fence, or just use a pathway to enclose it. Make sure the tallest flowers won't cover up your windows or doors. Modify the access paths so they branch off from the path near your front step or entry.

PLANTING ON A SHADY SITE If your site is in dappled sun or light shade (receiving about four hours of sun a day), you can use the Colonial Cottage Garden design with shade-tolerant perennials instead of perennials for full sun. In a lightly shaded site, the basic framework might include edgings of fragrant violets and lily-of-the-valley. Medium-height plants could include snowdrop anemones, bleeding hearts, and coral bells. Substitute hydrangeas or bush honeysuckles, which tolerate light shade, for the sun-loving roses, and plant astilbes instead of lavender. Then add other shade-tolerant easy-care perennials as you please, according to height. And remember to tuck in plenty of spring bulbs for early color!

PERENNIALS FOR A LIGHTLY SHADED COTTAGE GARDEN Try these cottage garden plants in a lightly shaded site that gets at least four hours of sun a day. They're arranged by height so you can see where they can fit into the garden. Plant clumps of three or more of each together and repeat plantings of the same plant in two or more beds. There is more information about how to grow each of these plants in Part 3 of this book.

Edging Plants	Grape hyacinths (*Muscari* spp.)	Woodland phlox (*Phlox divaricata*)	Lenten rose (*Helleborus orientalis*)
Allegheny foamflower (*Tiarella cordifolia*)	Grecian windflower (*Anemone blanda*)	Yellow corydalis (*Corydalis lutea*)	Snowdrop anemone (*Anemone sylvestris*)
Bethlehem sages (*Pulmonaria* spp.)	Lady's-mantle (*Alchemilla mollis*)	**Medium-Height Plants**	Virginia bluebells (*Mertensia virginica*)
Blood-red cranesbill (*Geranium sanguineum*)	Lily-of-the-valley (*Convallaria majalis*)	'Bridal Veil' astilbe (*Astilbe* x *arendsii* 'Bridal Veil')	**Showstopper Plants**
Bloodroot (*Sanguinaria canadensis*)	Siberian bugloss (*Brunnera macrophylla*)	Coral bells (*Heuchera* spp.)	Blue hosta (*Hosta ventricosa*)
Bugleweeds (*Ajuga* spp.)	Siberian squill (*Scilla siberica*)	Daffodils (*Narcissus* spp.)	'Cattleya' astilbe (*Astilbe* x *arendsii* 'Cattleya')
Canada wild ginger (*Asarum canadense*)	Tulips (*Tulipa greigii*)	Fortune's hosta (*Hosta fortunei*)	Daylilies (*Hemerocallis* spp.)
Crocuses (*Crocus* spp.)	Winter aconite (*Eranthis hyemalis*)	Fringed bleeding heart (*Dicentra eximia*)	Peppermint (*Mentha* x *piperita*)
Epimediums (*Epimedium* spp.)		Hardy geraniums (*Geranium* spp.)	Siberian iris (*Iris sibirica*)

COTTAGE GARDEN LORE Cottage garden plants are rich in history, hidden meanings, and mythical stories. This heritage makes your garden more than just a place to grow plants; it lets you bring the past to life. For example, plants played important roles in some ancient myths. And in Victorian times, people gave bouquets containing plants with special meanings as a way of passing messages. Choosing plants with a theme from folklore or history will make it even more fun to show friends and family around your garden. Time-travel now as you decide which plants to feature in your cottage garden.

Magical Plants

Tulips. The most lovely, fragrant, and long-lasting of the tulips are probably inhabited by pixies and their families, says old English lore. Check carefully before you dig these charmed bulbs up so you don't provoke pixie wrath.

Yarrow. Sturdy, aromatic yarrow once steeped in kettles of witches' brew. It's also an old-time remedy for soothing bloody noses and sores. Both uses led to the practice of hanging yarrow in a work shed, where it would magically repel thieves and be handy for treating cuts or scrapes. Although the magic may have gone out of yarrow, it still makes a fine cut flower.

▲ Yarrow

Flowers of Folklore and Myth

Anemones. Flexible-stemmed anemone flowers have long been linked to wind. An age-old question is whether a gentle breeze coaxes these windflowers to open as the stems bend and move. Ancient Greeks believed windflowers arose from the goddess Venus' tears, so anemones have long represented pain, suffering, and forsaken friends.

▲ Anemones

Daffodils. Sunny daffodils came by their botanical name of *Narcissus* from the myth of Narcissus, a Greek youth so handsome and vain that he fell in love with his reflection and took his own life in frustration. Where his blood fell, the first *Narcissus* sprang up.

Lily-of-the-valley. Irish lore claimed that fairies climbed lily-of-the-valley flowers like ladders. In Korea, the sword-shaped leaves were said to have arisen from drops of blood shed by a dragon-fighting giant.

Peony. The peony has a mixed folklore heritage. Ancient Greeks enjoyed it, finding magic in the glow of its moonlit flowers. Later Victorian sentimentalists, however, chastised the peony. To them, it meant anger and shame because of the blush of pink or red-flowered varieties.

Siberian irises. Siberian irises come in a sparkling spectrum of colors – blues, purples, yellows, white, and (thanks to recent breeding) red – justifying its age-old connection to Iris, Greek goddess of the rainbow. The iris assumed a royal lineage when it became part of Louis VII's coat of arms.

Flowers with Special Symbolism

Lavender. Lavender, an herb with a wonderful aroma, became a symbol of distrust in Victorian times. Perhaps the distrust is on the part of clothes moths and other pests that avoid sprigs set in dresser drawers! On a happier note, other early herbalists quilted lavender into a nightcap to set the mind at ease and encourage memory.

Lily-of-the-valley. The delicate but deliciously scented floral bells of lily-of-the-valley raised romantic notions of returning happiness in Victorian times.

▲ Tulips

Tulips. Tulips were the cause of rampant speculation and financial ruin in sixteenth-century Europe. But by Victorian times, tulips had been forgiven and had taken on the meaning "I love you."

Violets. Petite violets represented modesty in Victorian times, giving rise to the phrase "shrinking violet."

Useful Plants of Yesteryear

Iris. Roots of aromatic iris species have a rich violet aroma and have been used for fragrance or medicine since the time of the ancient Greeks. Today they flavor toothpaste and scent perfume.

Southernwood. The scented leaves of southernwood (*Artemisia abrotanum*) were used in folk medicine and treasured for keeping clean laundry smelling fresh (try it – it works!).

Violets. Violet petals, candied for desserts today as well as in historic times, were long reputed to soothe sore throats and coughs.

KEEPING YOUR COTTAGE GARDEN MANAGEABLE

After a season or two, some of the plants in your cottage garden may have spread too rambunctiously to suit you. That's when it's time to divide large clumps, thin overcrowded seedlings, remove plants growing in the wrong places, or open up space for new plants. When cutting back creeping plants, remove both the tops and roots. Be especially thorough with aggressive spreaders, such as mints or 'Silver King' artemisia. They can resprout from even tiny sections of root. If you work when the soil is moist, you may be able to uproot small plants just by grasping the base of the stem and pulling gently. But if the soil is hard or the plant is large, don't rely on hand-pulling. Use a small spade to dig around the plant or section of plant you want to remove and lever out a large ball of roots and soil. (For more on keeping spreading perennials under control, see page 130.)

To limit the spread of self-sowing perennials such as verbena, purple coneflower, and phlox, cut off the flowers as soon as they fade. If you want a few new seedlings, let one or two flowers mature and spread seeds. Uproot unwanted seedlings with a hoe, scraping the soil surface often when it's moist. To discourage new seeds from germinating, cover the soil with a layer of newspaper covered with organic mulch.

A DYNAMIC DRIVEWAY BORDER

Welcome everyone who enters your driveway with a bold border of easy-care perennials. Planting perennials along the driveway changes a necessary but unattractive feature of your yard into a terrific asset.

In the Dynamic Driveway Border, big clumps of ornamental grasses form the backbone of the garden, set off by groups of gold, pink, and white perennial flowers. The garden begins with low plants near the street, so you'll have a clear view of oncoming traffic when you pull out of the driveway. Then it builds in height with a mix of grasses, a rugosa rose, and bright perennials. As you pass by, the border gives the effect of a billowing field of changing color and texture.

▶ **In the early spring,** this border features bright yellow winter aconites, pink and white Spanish bluebells, and yellow and white crocuses.

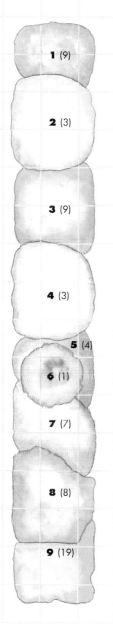

The Planting Plan. Many of the tall perennials in this border don't need staking as long as they have plenty of sun and moderately fertile soil. Some, like porcupine grass, will need simple grow-through supports. Set wire-grid supports over the plants in spring; they will grow through the grid and hide it from view. Leave the dried foliage of the grasses in place for winter interest; cut back their dried stems 4 to 6 inches above soil level in early spring. One long side of the Dynamic Driveway Border abuts the lawn. Edge it with a barrier to prevent lawn grasses from invading the bed.

1 'Herbstsonne' coneflower (*Rudbeckia nitida* 'Herbstsonne') with pink Spanish bluebells (*Hyacinthoides hispanicus*) and late-blooming yellow daffodils (*Narcissus* spp.)

2 Porcupine grass (*Miscanthus sinensis* var. *strictus*) with late-blooming bicolor daffodils and white Spanish bluebells

3 'David' phlox (*Phlox paniculata* 'David') with *Tulipa pulchella* 'Persian Pearl'

4 'Adagio' Japanese silver grass (*Miscanthus sinensis* 'Adagio') with midseason yellow daffodils and yellow crocuses (*Crocus* spp.)

5 'Biokovo' cranesbill (*Geranium* 'Biokovo')

6 'Magnifica' rugosa rose (*Rosa rugosa* 'Magnifica')

7 'Karl Foerster' feather reed grass (*Calamagrostis* x *acutiflora* 'Karl Foerster') with midseason bicolor daffodils and white crocuses

8 'Moonbeam' coreopsis (*Coreopsis verticillata* 'Moonbeam') with winter aconite (*Eranthis hyemalis*)

9 'Bees' Ruby' thrift (*Armeria* 'Bees' Ruby')

Design by Bobbie Schwartz
( ) = number of plants to plant

▢ = 3½ feet

▶ **As fall arrives,** 'Herbstsonne' coneflowers, coreopsis, and rugosa roses continue blooming strongly. The rippling plumes of the ornamental grasses fill the border with intriguing sights and sounds.

GARDENS FOR SHORT AND LONG DRIVEWAYS The Dynamic Driveway Border is designed for a 50-foot driveway, but chances are your driveway isn't precisely 50 feet. If it's shorter, adapt the plan by planting fewer plants of each type. For example, cut back the number of phlox and coreopsis from nine to seven or five. Keep in mind that odd numbers of plants in each clump tend to produce a more natural look. That's because when you plant an even number of plants, you'll be tempted to set them in formal squares or rectangles that won't look right with this design.

To extend the border for a longer driveway, repeat some of the groups of perennials. You might, for instance, expand the midsection of the border – repeating the 'Karl Foerster' feather reed grass, 'Biokovo' cranesbill, rugosa rose, and Japanese silver grass sequence to add an extra 20 feet. Or, you can expand the size of each cluster of perennials. Instead of using only 9 'Moonbeam' coreopsis or 'David' phlox, enlarge that planting to 11 or 13. To add 4 feet with a single plant, add another large *Miscanthus*.

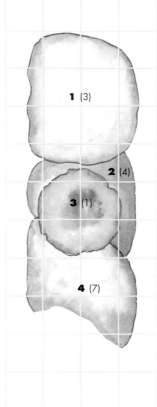

EXTEND THE BORDER

For a longer driveway you can repeat the midsection of the border to add an extra 20 feet.

1 'Adagio' Japanese silver grass (*Miscanthus sinensis* 'Adagio') with midseason yellow daffodils and yellow crocuses (*Crocus* spp.)

2 'Biokovo' cranesbill (*Geranium* 'Biokovo')

3 'Magnifica' rugosa rose (*Rosa rugosa* 'Magnifica')

4 'Karl Foerster' feather reed grass (*Calamagrostis* x *acutiflora* 'Karl Foerster') with midseason bicolor daffodils and white crocuses

▶ **A wooden fence** edged with a groundcover makes a nice border for a rustic driveway. Plant tall perennials like blue false indigo behind the fence for added interest.

CREATING A WIDE BORDER If you'd like even more of a good thing, you can expand the Dynamic Driveway Border from 6 to 9 feet wide. This allows you to add another layer of low-growing perennials all along the edges of the driveway. Here are some ideas to try:

- Move the tall 'Herbstsonne' coneflowers back and plant blue salvia in the foreground.
- Plant sea-pink (*Armeria maritima*) in front of the 'David' phlox and add another rugosa rose in the background.
- Move the rugosa rose back, set 'Moonbeam' coreopsis at its feet, and add more 'Biokovo' cranesbill as an edging.
- Beside the street, use blue salvia behind sweeps of sea-pink and 'Moonbeam' coreopsis.

PLANTING ALONG A SHADY DRIVEWAY If you have shade trees planted alongside your driveway, the Dynamic Driveway Border just won't work for your site. But you can perk up a row of trees—and cut down on tricky mowing—by planting perennial ground-covers under the trees right up to the edge of the

◀ **Soften the edge** of a driveway or path by planting sweeps of graceful perennials like this salvia alongside.

driveway. Bugleweeds (*Ajuga* spp.) and epimediums (*Epimedium* spp.) are both good choices. Try interplanting ferns or spring bulbs for added color and texture.

◀ **Mix hostas** with variegated leaves and different leaf colors to make a distinctive edging for a shady driveway.

GREETING GARDENS If you're not ready to plunge into planting a border to span your entire driveway, try planting a smaller "greeting garden" instead. By carefully choosing a small group of easy-care perennials, you can create a charming garden that will brighten the entrance of your driveway or a spot by your front door all season long.

◀ A Shady Hosta Garden

Here's a chance to plant your favorite hosta, or a great excuse to buy a special new cultivar you've been longing for! The handsome hosta foliage is a season-long central feature of this grouping. The Solomon's seal and Bethlehem sage foliage will also be an asset from spring through fall, as well as provide a lovely show of spring flowers.

- Squills (*Scilla* spp.)
- 'Mrs. Moon' Bethlehem sage (*Pulmonaria saccharata* 'Mrs. Moon')
- Hosta (*Hosta* species or cultivar)
- Variegated Solomon's seal (*Polygonatum odoratum* 'Variegatum')

▶ A Shady Garden with Ferns

The delicate flowers of violets and foamflowers look cool and inviting in this elegant grouping. The silver-flecked leaves of the Japanese painted fern are lovely from spring through fall, while the black snakeroot flower spikes add a dramatic touch in summer.

- Violets (*Viola* spp.)
- Foamflowers (*Tiarella* spp.)
- Japanese painted fern (*Athyrium goeringianum* 'Pictum')
- Black snakeroot (*Cimicifuga racemosa*)

◀ A Silvery Sunny Garden

This quartet proves that you don't need a fancy plant list for a great garden. The arching stems of Russian sage and gorgeous silvery artemisia foliage make this garden a pleasure to view all season long. Grape hyacinths provide spring cheer and then go dormant. Airy blue flower sprays of Russian sage bloom in summer, and bold royal purple New England asters follow in the fall.

- Grape hyacinths
  (*Muscari* spp.)
- 'Nana' silvermound artemisia
  (*Artemisia schmidtiana* 'Nana')
- Russian sage
  (*Perovskia atriplicifolia*)
- 'Purple Dome' New England aster
  (*Aster novae-angliae* 'Purple Dome')

▶ A Multicolored Sunny Garden

Daffodils and blue bugleweed flowers get this minigarden off to a great spring start. Coreopsis, Frikart's aster, and iris supply the summer color. After the iris flowers fade, its spiky leaves add interest into fall, while the coreopsis and aster keep right on blooming. And throughout the season, crinkled, glossy bugleweed foliage is an eye-catching accent.

- Assorted daffodils
  (five or seven bulbs of each cultivar)
  (*Narcissus* spp.)
- 'Metallica Crispa' bugleweed
  (*Ajuga pyramidalis* 'Metallica Crispa')
- 'Moonbeam' coreopsis
  (*Coreopsis verticillata* 'Moonbeam')
- Frikart's aster
  (*Aster* x *frikartii*)
- Blue or purple Siberian iris
  (*Iris sibirica*)

A Butterfly and Hummingbird Garden

What's better than a garden of beautiful perennials?
A garden of beautiful perennials with butterflies and hummingbirds in it!

You can attract butterflies by planting fragrant flowers, especially tube-shaped flowers such as violet sage. Butterflies also love clusters of small flowers like those of butterfly weed and asters. Hummingbirds are attracted to red and other bright blossoms, particularly trumpet-shaped flowers they can slip their beaks into. A perennial garden that caters to butterflies and hummingbirds bursts with color, especially in summer, when it is at the height of bloom.

▼ **In late summer,**
the pink flowers of 'Autumn Joy' sedum open, deepening to crimson and rust in fall and winter. Black-eyed Susans, violet sage, and purple coneflowers add to the splendor. Tall pink 'Alma Potschke' asters are another highlight that will last into fall.

The Planting Plan. This border offers great close-up views of hummingbirds and butterflies in action. The garden needs full sun, so give it a site on the south or west side of your home. One special hummingbird- and butterfly-attracting perennial featured in this garden is anise hyssop, which has fragrant foliage and blue flowers and blooms from summer through fall. It grows 2 to 3 feet tall, is hardy in Zones 4 to 8, and is easy to grow.

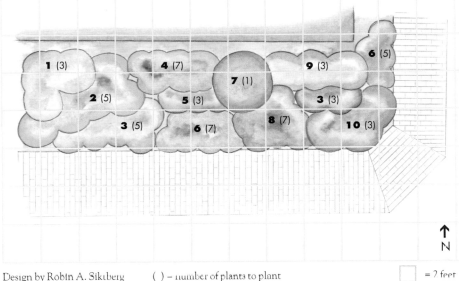

Design by Robin A. Siktberg   ( ) – number of plants to plant   ☐ = 2 feet

↑ N

1 Anise hyssop
(*Agastache foeniculum*)

2 'Magnus' purple coneflower (*Echinacea purpurea* 'Magnus')

3 'Goldsturm' black-eyed Susan (*Rudbeckia fulgida* 'Goldsturm')

4 'Lucifer' crocosmia (*Crocosmia* 'Lucifer')

5 'Kobold' spike gayfeather (*Liatris spicata* 'Kobold')

6 'East Friesland' sage (*Salvia* x *superba* 'East Friesland')

7 Blue false indigo (*Baptisia australis*)

8 Butterfly weed (*Asclepias tuberosa*)

9 'Alma Potschke' New England aster (*Aster novae-angliae* 'Alma Potschke')

10 'Autumn Joy' sedum (*Sedum* 'Autumn Joy')

▼**Blue and purple** predominate in early summer in this garden, with violet sage and blue false indigo in flower. A trio of anise hyssop plants cluster beside the patio, where you can easily enjoy their licorice-scented leaves and spikes of blue flowers.

▶ **To catch a humming-bird's eye** early in the season, include spring-blooming bleeding heart in your garden.

▼ **Butterflies love** lavender Frikart's aster, so use it in place of brassy blooms like butterfly weed.

EDGING THE GARDEN You'll want to stroll alongside your butterfly and hummingbird garden often to enjoy visiting with your winged friends. You can edge the garden with a red brick walk that echoes the warm reds and pinks of the crocosmias and asters. Or, for a softer effect, lay a walkway of neutral gray flagstones.

A COOL-COLOR BUTTERFLY GARDEN If hot colors don't suit your style, plant a more subtle butterfly garden substituting blue and lavender flowers for the bold red and orange. For example, you could leave out crocosmia and plant Russian sage (*Perovskia atriplicifolia*), which has lovely, mistlike sprays of blue flowers in summer that mature to form attractive seedheads in fall. Replace butterfly weed with Frikart's aster (*Aster frikartii*), a loose, bushy perennial that sports masses of lavender daisylike flowers from summer into fall.

A PLANT MENU FOR HUMMINGBIRDS Don't limit yourself to the plants featured in the Butterfly and Hummingbird Garden design when planting for hummingbirds. They will feed from a wide variety of annuals, perennials, shrubs, and vines. Red or pink flowers are sure to draw hungry hummers. (They may also be attracted to some orange, white, violet, blue, and yellow flowers, like honeysuckle.)

Annuals. There are plenty of brightly colored annuals to draw hummingbirds. Cannas (*Canna* × *generalis*) are large showy flowers that bloom in mid- to late summer in red, pink, orange, and yellow. Annual salvia (*Salvia splendens*) has fiery red flowers all season long. Nasturtiums, flowering tobacco (*Nicotiana alata*), and petunias are common bedding plants that hummers love.

Perennials. Among the easy-care perennials covered in Part 3 that attract hummingbirds are bleeding hearts (*Dicentra* spp.), coral bells (*Heuchera sanguinea*), and phlox. Some other perennials you may want to try include two lovely wildflowers: wild columbine (*Aquilegia canadensis*), which is hardy from Zones 3 to 8, and cardinal flower (*Lobelia cardinalis*), which is hardy from Zones 2 to 9. Torch lilies (*Kniphofia* spp.) produce stunning torchlike flowers in late spring and summer and are hardy from Zones 5 to 9. Bee balms (*Monarda* spp.) are lively summer bloomers, but they need evenly moist soil and are prone to powdery mildew unless you choose a resistant cultivar like 'Marshall's Delight'.

Trees, Shrubs, and Vines. If you've fallen head over heels in love with hummers, branch out into planting woody plants that attract them. Fruit trees (including ornamental types) that attract hummingbirds include apple, cherry, peach, plum, and citrus. Hummers will visit rhododendrons and lilacs. They also love a flowering vine called trumpet creeper (*Campsis radicans*) that has orange or red trumpet-shaped flowers and is hardy from Zones 4 to 9. Also try glossy abelia (*Abelia* × *grandiflora*), a shrub with lightly fragrant tubular white flowers that is hardy from Zones 6 to 10.

A BACKGROUND PATH The Butterfly and Hummingbird Garden design is 6 feet deep, which allows it to include several interesting plant combinations. It's fairly easy to maintain a border of this depth with a hoe or other long-handled tool. But

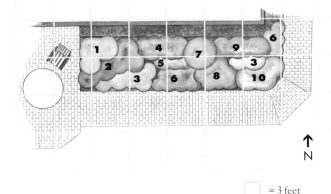

↑
N

☐ = 3 feet

if you have trouble reaching across a 6-foot-wide bed to weed or trim flowers, plan for a 1-foot-wide access path along the rear of the garden, as shown in the plan above. Once the garden fills in, the pathway will be nearly invisible. Leaving a bare area at the back of the garden is also a good idea if you have overhanging eaves that block rainfall from the soil below them. (Refer to page 53 for the list of plants.)

KEEPING YOUR GARDEN COLORFUL You can interplant spring-flowering bulbs with the perennials in the Butterfly and Hummingbird Garden so it will be colorful and enjoyable even if the butterflies aren't out yet. Work clusters of daffodils, tulips, squills, crocus, and grape hyacinths between clumps of perennials. Bulbs work especially well near blue false indigo and butterfly weed. These two perennials may never need to be divided, so there's no risk the bulbs will be damaged by digging.

To keep your garden from looking barren in the winter, when all the perennials are dormant, leave the seedheads of purple coneflowers, black-eyed Susans, and 'Autumn Joy' sedum in place. They'll provide interesting color and texture until spring returns again.

CHANGING THE LOCATION If you can't find the right spot for the Butterfly and Hummingbird Garden near your house, try it in front of a hedge or wall instead. You could plant it along a walkway or even at the edge of your property. (It might encourage you to get more exercise – a daily nature observation walk!)

GROW A BUTTERFLY NURSERY You and your family can witness one of nature's most miraculous transformations in your own yard: the metamorphosis of a caterpillar into a butterfly. To increase your chances of seeing this miracle, start a butterfly nursery of plants that butterfly caterpillars can eat. Then you can enjoy the spectacle of watching the caterpillars grow, form a chrysalis, and emerge as beautiful butterflies. Your nursery may range from a small patch of clover to a grove of trees, depending on the type of butterflies you're interested in observing. Caterpillars have specific food choices, including the following:

Giant swallowtail larvae – Citrus trees
Monarch larvae – Milkweeds (*Asclepias* spp.), including butterfly weed
Mourning cloak larvae – Willows (*Salix* spp.), poplars (*Populus* spp.), birches (*Betula* spp.), and other deciduous trees
Painted lady larvae – Many kinds of wildflowers
Silvery blue larvae – Legumes
Some types of sulphur larvae – Clover
Some types of swallowtail larvae – Fennel and dill
Spicebush swallowtail larvae – Spicebush (*Lindera benzoin*), sassafras (*Sassafras albidum*), or tulip tree (*Liriodendron tulipifera*)

▲ **Colorful caterpillars** can turn into black swallowtails or other beautiful butterflies.

MAKE A HUMMINGBIRD FEEDER The best way to keep an active flock of hummingbirds in your garden is to feed them – throughout the growing season in cool climates or year-round in warm climates. This usually means supplementing your hummingbird flowers with a hummingbird feeder. They're inexpensive to buy or, if you enjoy homemade projects, easy to make yourself (see the directions below).

If you set up more than one feeder, separate them by at least 6 feet. If your feeders are too close together, one hummingbird may dominate them and chase other birds away. Once hummingbirds discover your feeders, keep them filled so the birds can rely on them. Put your feeders out year after year; migrating birds will return expecting to find them in place. You can buy premade hummingbird feeders at home-and-garden stores or through mail-order catalogs.

All feeders contain a nectar reservoir. You can make your own nectar or buy premade brands. To make your own, mix a sugar solution of 4 or 5 parts water to 1 part white sugar. Do not add red food coloring to the nectar – it's not good for the hummingbirds. It's better to add red to the outside of the feeder to attract them. Boil the mixture for 5 minutes to dissolve the sugar and sterilize the solution. You can refrigerate any extra for seven days. Keep the nectar fresh and the feeder clean so it won't mold or mildew and make the hummingbirds sick. Wash the feeder every couple of days and refill with fresh nectar daily. It helps to place the feeder in shade so the nectar is less likely to ferment. Wipe off the outside of the feeder regularly with a damp cloth to discourage bees and yellow jackets.

Step-by-Step Feeder Making

1 Buy a small glass or plastic guinea pig or hamster water bottle. This will be the nectar reservoir.

2 Fashion a wire harness that fits around the bottle so the bottle can dangle upside down from a post or tree branch, with the metal drinking spout protruding horizontally.

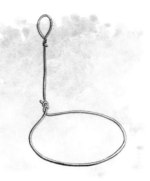

3 Glue a red plastic flower to the reservoir near the spout.

4 Fill the reservoir with cooled nectar made from 4 or 5 parts water to 1 part white sugar.

Hang a hummingbird feeder by your favorite sitting area so you can enjoy watching these acrobatic birds at work.

COPING WITH PEST PROBLEMS When you invite butterflies and hummingbirds into your garden, using sprays – even organic sprays like pyrethrins – is out of the question. Instead, use nontoxic methods that target pest insects and leave butterflies and caterpillars free to enjoy your perennials.

◀ **To fight aphids** without using pesticides, plant yarrow and leave a few weeds like dandelions and Queen-Anne's-lace to attract aphid-eating lady beetles.

● If you find pest insects on your perennials, pick them off by hand, and kill them by dropping them into a bucket of warm, soapy water. If butterfly caterpillars are eating your perennials *too* enthusiastically, carefully handpick them off the plants and move them to an out-of-the-way place.

● Encourage beneficial insects and animals to help with pest control. Butterfly-attracting perennials also attract many insects that prey on pests. You can also put an overturned flowerpot with a hole cut in the side in your garden to shelter a pest-eating toad.

● If aphids are a problem, you can kill them by aiming the hose at the affected plants and spraying them with a strong stream of water.

● Japanese beetles can make a mess of the foliage of some perennials. Instead of spraying the beetles, apply beneficial nematodes (sold as Biosafe) to your lawn. These microscopic organisms attack and kill white grubs, the larvae of the beetles, but do not harm caterpillars or butterflies.

● Leave some pests in your flowers for the hummingbirds to eat.

A WONDERFUL WILDFLOWER GARDEN

If you want a beautiful easy-care perennial garden with the added bonus of birds and butterflies, try planting wildflowers.

Perennial wildflowers are tough plants that are accustomed to surviving without any pampering, making them a terrific choice for easy-care gardens. And many wildflowers that are native to the United States are the natural food sources for our native birds and butterflies. Plant the wildflowers, and the wildlife will come.

The key to successful wildflower gardens is to plant wildflowers in soil and light conditions that closely match those of their native habitats. For example, black snakeroot (*Cimicifuga racemosa*) grows wild along the margins of rich woodlands, so it needs a lightly shaded site with moist soil incorporating lots of organic matter. In contrast, gayfeathers (*Liatris* spp.) are prairie natives that need full sun and an average, well-drained soil.

▼ **Plant this wildflower garden** at the back of your property or anywhere you have mature trees. A mulched walkway meanders through the garden, and a narrower path cuts into the shady area so you can get a close-up view of delicate woodland wildflowers. Low-growing flowers stretch beside the paths and in the front of the garden.

The Planting Plan. This garden combines woodland wildflowers and sunny meadow wildflowers around oak trees. The shade-loving flowers nestle under the oaks, with the sun-lovers at the fringes, beyond the spread of the trees' branches. You'll need to decide for yourself how many plants of each type to plant. See "How Many Perennials Should You Buy?" on page 79 for guidance.

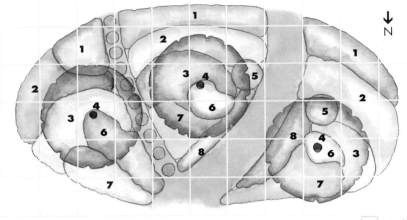

Design by Susan McClure

☐ = 3¼ feet

1 Tall meadow and prairie wildflowers

2 Medium-height meadow and prairie wildflowers

3 Shade-loving perennials and foliage plants

4 Oak tree

5 Black snakeroot (*Cimicifuga racemosa*)

6 Lady fern (*Athyrium filix-femina*)

7 Low-growing woodland wildflowers

8 Wild blue phlox (*Phlox divaricata*), creeping phlox (*P. stolonifera*), and violets (*Viola* spp.)

Low-Growing Woodland Wildflowers

Allegheny foamflower (*Tiarella cordifolia*)

Bloodroot (*Sanguinaria canadensis*)

Canada wild ginger (*Asarum canadense*)

Dutchman's breeches (*Dicentra cucullaria*)

Squirrel corn (*Dicentra canadensis*)

Wild bleeding heart (*Dicentra eximia*)

Shade-Loving Perennials and Foliage Plants

Solomon's seal (*Polygonatum biflorum*)

Virginia bluebells (*Mertensia virginica*)

Wild cranesbill (*Geranium maculatum*)

Virginia bluebells

PERENNIALS FOR THE WONDERFUL WILDFLOWER

GARDEN In nature, wildflowers sprout and grow where the conditions suit them best, creating their own patterns and combinations. To re-create that effect in your garden, avoid planting in formal rows or groups. Pick the plants you like best from those listed here, and plant in random clumps or groupings. Over time, as some plants naturally spread or reseed themselves, the garden will become its own designer.

You may wonder how many plants to buy to fill your garden. That depends on which plants you choose. Check to find out the mature height and spread of the plants you've selected. Plant small perennials 12 to 18 inches apart. Space plants with a spreading habit 18 to 24 inches apart. For large meadow perennials such as Joe-Pye weed, you may want to space the plants up to 4 feet apart.

Medium-Height Meadow and Prairie Wildflowers

Bigflower coreopsis (*Coreopsis grandiflora*)

Black-eyed Susans (*Rudbeckia* spp.)

Butterfly weed (*Asclepias tuberosa*)

Purple coneflower (*Echinacea purpurea*)

Tall gayfeather (*Liatris scariosa*)

Tall Meadow and Prairie Wildflowers

Joe-Pye weed (*Eupatorium fistulosum*)

New England aster (*Aster novae-angliae*)

▶ **Try mixing** meadow wildflowers like orange butterfly weed and yellow black-eyed Susans with annuals like blue-flowered larkspur for cheerful, eye-catching combinations.

MORE WAYS TO USE WILDFLOWERS Even if you don't have space in your yard for a woodland or meadow garden, you can still plant perennial wildflowers. Meadow and prairie wildflowers look lovely in a sunny border alongside traditional perennials like peonies. You can even plant wildflowers in a formal foundation bed. Their lively colors and graceful forms add life and beauty to almost any garden.

If you have a small yard with just a single shade tree, try a miniplanting of woodland wildflowers. A small meadow, measuring about 10 square yards, of purple coneflowers, gayfeathers, and rudbeckias can add the care-free feeling of a wildflower garden to your yard.

CHOOSING WILDFLOWERS FOR YOUR CLIMATE

The wildflowers used in the Wonderful Wildflower Garden are recommended for cool, temperate climates like those found in Zones 2 through 6. You can check whether they are suitable for your region by checking Part 3 of this book, or talking to plant experts at a local botanical garden, native plant society, or other conservation group. You may need to substitute wildflowers that are native to your area to produce a truly easy-care garden.

MATCHING THE GARDEN TO YOUR YARD If your yard doesn't have mature trees, try one of these options for adapting the garden to your site.

Planting under an Arbor. To make a garden without shade trees, you can cultivate woodland wildflowers under an arbor like the one shown on page 30. Or you can eliminate the shade plants altogether and use the sun-loving plants to make a meadow or prairie garden.

Downsizing the Garden. To make the garden smaller, eliminate the tall sun-loving plants and use fewer of the medium-height shade plants.

Increasing the Size of the Planting. To make the garden larger, increase the size of any of the individual plant groups, remembering to match the size of the groups to the size of your sunny and shady areas.

Planting Plan Variation. For a smaller garden, try planting just one section of the Wonderful Wildflower Garden design. You'll still plant a mix of sun- and shade-loving wildflowers and ferns.

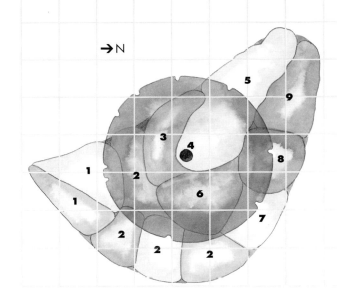

1 Tall meadow and prairie wildflowers

2 Medium-height meadow and prairie wildflowers

3 Solomon's seal (*Polygonatum biflorum*)

4 Oak tree

5 Lady fern (*Athyrium filix-femina*)

6 Virginia bluebells (*Mertensia virginica*)

7 Wild cranesbill (*Geranium maculatum*)

8 Bleeding hearts (*Dicentra* spp.)

9 Allegheny foamflower (*Tiarella cordifolia*)

▼ **This small wildflower garden** is lovely in the spring when Virginia bluebells, Allegheny foamflowers, wild cranesbill, and bleeding hearts bloom.

TAKING CUES FROM MOTHER NATURE In the Wonderful Wildflower Garden, plants that need similar soil conditions and light levels grow in informal groups, just as they would in nature. This produces variety and delightful surprises. To have a thriving wildflower garden, be sure you've prepared the soil to match the natural habitats of the plants.

Preparing for Woodland Wildflowers. You can create a woodland wildflower garden beneath shade trees in your yard by adding lots of shredded leaves to mimic a natural woodland where leaves collect and decay year after year. For best results, site the garden under deep-rooted shade trees, such as oaks, where small flowers can grow freely without competition from aggressive woody roots.

▲ **When planting under a tree** that's surrounded by lawn, leave a 6- to 8-foot-diameter ring around the trunk unplanted to help keep the tree healthy.

If your soil is naturally rich with lots of decayed leaves, it may be suitable for a woodland garden as is. For other soils, add a 4- to 6-inch-deep layer of composted leaves before planting. If the soil is poor or riddled with tree roots, you may want to create a raised planting bed up to 4 inches thick by blending layers of 1 inch of coarse sand, 1 inch of topsoil, and 2 inches of compost. Don't pile soil right against the tree trunks. Instead, try planting ferns near the trunks in the gaps between the roots.

Most woodland wildflowers prefer moist soil. If your site is dry, especially during peak growth in spring and early summer, install a trickle irrigation system as described on page 83.

Preparing for Meadow Wildflowers. To ready a site for a sunny meadow garden, strip off any sod, loosen the soil, and carefully pull or dig out all perennial weed roots. Add a 2-inch layer of compost and turn it into the soil with a rotary tiller or digging fork. Let the soil settle for a couple of weeks, then hoe off all newly sprouted weeds. Continue to scrape the soil with a hoe weekly until few weeds resprout. After planting, mulch open areas with newspaper covered by organic mulch.

▲ **To strip sod** off the site for your wildflower garden, use a sharp spade to cut through the roots.

SPECIAL CARE FOR WILDFLOWERS

Woodland Gardens. Replenish organic matter in woodland gardens annually in spring to keep the soil moist and rich. In fall, rake off leaves that pile up more than 2 inches deep, because they could smother young plants. Compost the extra leaves.

Meadow Gardens. Some gardeners like to leave meadow garden plants in place through the winter so they can enjoy the shapes and colors of the dried foliage and seedpods. It's often easiest to mow down a meadow planting with a lawnmower set on a high setting. Mow the entire garden in fall or wait to mow until early spring. Remove the dried stems or cut them up in small pieces and scatter as mulch. In late spring, cut back the new growth of tall perennials by one-third to keep them from flopping. If plant growth is very slow or poor, fertilize your meadow garden in the spring with a balanced organic fertilizer.

PROPAGATING WILDFLOWERS Once you discover how easy it is to grow perennial wildflowers, you may want to add more of them in your yard or introduce your gardening friends to their charm. Two great ways to create more wildflowers are to dig and divide existing plants and to collect seeds and sow them yourself.

Making Divisions. You can propagate spring wildflowers by dividing the root clumps as the plants begin to go dormant in summer or fall. For ferns and summer- and fall-blooming meadow and prairie plants, the best time to divide is in spring, as the shoots first emerge. For detailed directions on dividing perennials, see "Dividends of Dividing" on page 86.

▲ **Plant small divisions** in 6-inch pots in a soil mix containing 1 part peat-based potting mix and 2 parts woodland soil.

If the divisions from your perennials are large and have plenty of roots, you can replant them directly in the garden. Put small divisions in pots. Keep spring divisions in the pots for about six weeks; fall divisions should stay in the pots in a protected spot until the following spring.

Starting from Seed. Another way to propagate wildflowers is by collecting their seeds and sowing them either indoors or outdoors. In fact, if you have wildflowers already growing on your property, you can collect the seeds and use them to start your wildflower garden.

You may wonder whether to collect wildflower seeds or plants from the woods or other wild areas in your neighborhood or in parks. Please *don't* collect seeds from

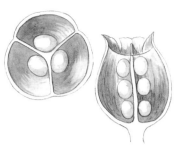

▲ **Remove wildflower seeds** from the seedpods before sowing them in pots or in the garden.

the wild. You may damage the natural balance in the spot where you collect, leading to the demise of the entire wild population at that spot. It's always better to buy plants or seeds from reputable sources than to risk causing damage.

When you collect seeds from your own plants, be sure to wait until the seeds are ripe. You'll find the seeds inside berries or dried pods. Remove any clinging bits of berry or pod, and sow several seeds in a 4- or 6-inch pot. Use the peat soil potting blend described in the caption at left for woodland wildflowers; for prairie wildflowers, use a peat-based seed-starting mix.

The seeds of most wild-flowers from areas that have cold winters require a period of cold, moist temperatures or alternating

▲ **Using a metal file** or knife to scratch the seedcoat can help some wildflower seeds germinate faster.

cold and warm periods to encourage germination in the spring. You can meet this need by leaving the pots of seeds outdoors all through the winter or until the seedlings germinate. There are still other seeds that may need scarification, a slight nicking of the seedcoat, to stimulate germination. You can do this with a knife for large seeds or by shaking small seeds in a jar containing a piece of sandpaper. To find out the specific temperature or scarification treatment needed for individual species of wildflowers, consult one of the references listed in "Recommended Reading" on page 155.

A FABULOUS
FOUR-SEASON GARDEN

An inviting garden at your front door offers a wonderful welcome to guests.
It also gives you and your family a pleasant and colorful view to enjoy every day.

Don't let stodgy evergreens surround your entryway! Use perennials to say a cheerful hello and create a beautiful scene all year long.

This contemporary entryway garden for a lightly shaded site features a walkway leading past blocks of perennials that combine handsome foliage and flowers for great year-round color and interest. On the opposite side of the walkway, a mixed planting of shrubs and perennials gives the scene greater impact and extra off-season color and interest.

▼ **In the spring,** the Fabulous Four-Season Garden features white foamflowers, Lenten roses, tulips interplanted with wild bleeding heart, yellow corydalis, and the lovely blossoms of 'Spring Glory' serviceberry.

The Planting Plan. The square-grid planting system used for this design makes the garden extra-easy to plant and tend. Self-sown corydalis seedlings will pop up in neighboring squares; watch for them and pull them out before they get too weedy. Prune any dead or broken branches from the woody plants as needed to keep them healthy and attractive. For the pots of annuals, use caladium, yellow coleus, fuchsia, and pink impatiens.

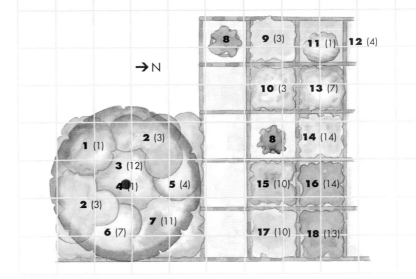

→ N

Design by Bobbie Schwartz   ( ) = number of plants to plant   ☐ = 3 feet

1 Oakleaf hydrangea (*Hydrangea quercifolia*)

2 Coast leucothoe (*Leucothoe axillaris*)

3 'Sulphureum' Persian epimedium (*Epimedium × versicolor* 'Sulphureum')

4 'Spring Glory' serviceberry (*Amelanchier canadensis* 'Spring Glory')

5 'Hyperion' daylily (*Hemerocallis* 'Hyperion')

6 Lady's-mantle (*Alchemilla mollis*)

7 Chinese astilbe (*Astilbe chinensis* var. *pumila*) with winter aconite (*Eranthis hyemalis*)

8 Potted annuals

9 'Angustifolius' Christmas rose (*Helleborus niger* 'Angustifolius') with golden crocus (*Crocus chrysanthus*)

10 Lenten rose (*Helleborus orientalis*)

11 'Krossa Regal' hosta (*Hosta* 'Krossa Regal') with 'King Alfred' type daffodil (*Narcissus* 'Dutch Master' and others) and Siberian squill (*Scilla siberica*)

12 'Professor van der Weilen' astilbe (*Astilbe thunbergii* 'Professor van der Weilen') with 'Silver Chimes' daffodil (*Narcissus* 'Silver Chimes')

13 'Laird of Skye' foamflower (*Tiarella* 'Laird of Skye')

14 Yellow corydalis (*Corydalis lutea*)

15 'Palace Purple' heuchera (*Heuchera* 'Palace Purple')

16 'Fuji Blue' balloon flower (*Platycodon grandiflorus* 'Fuji Blue') with Spanish bluebells (*Hyacinthoides hispanicus*)

17 Cranesbill (*Geranium renardii*)

18 Wild bleeding heart (*Dicentra eximia*) with 'Lilac Wonder' tulip (*Tulipa bakeri* 'Lilac Wonder')

◀ **Foliage colors** and textures are the main features of interest in the fall garden. Oakleaf hydrangea blossoms and the red foliage of the serviceberry are highlights.

A SUNNY ENTRYWAY GARDEN If your entryway garden faces to the south, it is probably in full sun all day. You can adapt the Fabulous Four-Season Garden to your site by planting sun-loving perennials in place of the shade-loving perennials in the design. Just use the list below with the planting plan shown on page 65.

1 Oakleaf hydrangea (*Hydrangea quercifolia*)

2 Coast leucothoe (*Leucothoe axillaris*)

3 'Sulphureum' Persian epimedium (*Epimedium* x *versicolor* 'Sulphureum')

4 'Spring Glory' serviceberry (*Amelanchier canadensis* 'Spring Glory')

5 'Hyperion' daylily (*Hemerocallis* 'Hyperion')

6 Lady's-mantle (*Alchemilla mollis*)

7 Chinese astilbe (*Astilbe chinensis* var. *pumila*) with winter aconite (*Eranthis hyemalis*)

8 Potted annuals

9 Adam's-needle (*Yucca filamentosa*) with golden crocus (*Crocus chrysanthus*)

10 'Autumn Joy' sedum (*Sedum* 'Autumn Joy')

11 'Krossa Regal' hosta (*Hosta* 'Krossa Regal') with 'King Alfred' type daffodil (*Narcissus* 'Dutch Master' and others) and Siberian squill (*Scilla siberica*)

12 Russian sage *Perovskia atriplicifolia* with 'Silver Chimes' daffodil (*Narcissus* 'Silver Chimes'

13 'Album' blood-red cranesbill (*Geranium sanguineum* 'Album')

14 'Moonbeam' coreopsis (*Coreopsis verticillata* 'Moonbeam')

15 'Palace Purple' heuchera (*Heuchera* 'Palace Purple')

16 'Fuji Blue' balloon flower (*Platycodon grandiflorus* 'Fuji Blue') with Spanish bluebells (*Hyacinthoides hispanicus*)

17 Cranesbill (*Geranium renardii*)

18 Pink tickseed (*Coreopsis rosea*) with 'Lilac Wonder' tulip (*Tulipa bakeri* 'Lilac Wonder')

▶ **'Golden Sword'** Adam's needle (*Yucca filamentosa* 'Golden Sword') is a bold accent plant for a four-season garden in a sunny location.

Changing the Layout. Many houses don't have a corner nook like the one shown in the Fabulous Four-Season Garden. However, you can adapt the garden to suit almost any house shape. Here, for example, the garden around the 'Spring Glory' serviceberry is planted to the right of the perennials along the pathway, providing a lovely backdrop that frames the perennials like a picture. If you have a shady site, use this layout with the plant list on page 65; if your site is sunny, refer to the list of plants on page 66 instead.

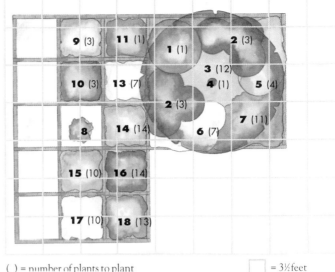

( ) = number of plants to plant   □ = 3½ feet

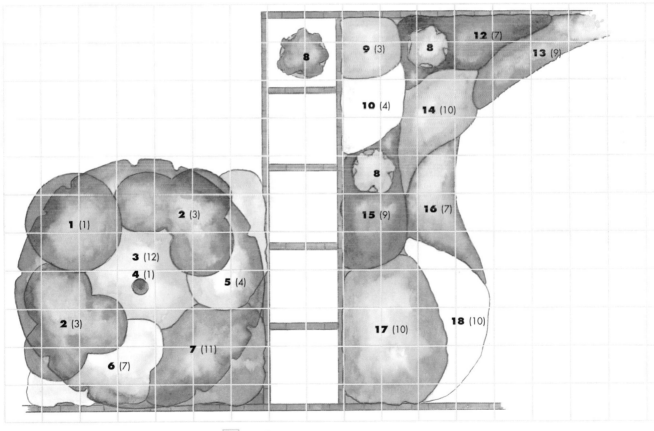

( ) = number of plants to plant   □ = 1¼ feet

A Casual Entry Garden. The block layout of the Fabulous Four-Season Garden may not match all house styles. And if you prefer informal gardens, it just may not match *you*! For a more relaxed approach, change the planting grid to a gentle S-curve bed as shown here. If you have a shady site, use this layout with the plant list on page 65; if your site is sunny, refer to the list of plants on page 66 instead.

USING GARDEN ART FOR FOUR-SEASON INTEREST It's not easy to create a four-season garden with perennials alone, because most of them die back or get cut back as winter approaches. Woody plants like shrubs and trees offer winter interest with colorful bark or their branch pattern. But if you don't have space to plant trees or shrubs, or want an instant effect, try garden art for year-round interest. While not "natural," sculpture and gardens work well together and are fun too!

Garden art is very popular, so you're bound to find something that suits your taste and budget. Animal or wildlife statues are naturals for gardens. If you like an old-fashioned look, consider antiques such as old water pumps, wagon wheels, or ceramic planters. Sundials and pedestal-mounted gazing balls are classic options. For contemporary gardens, look for modern art such as stone or metal sculptures.

▲ **A birdbath is a sure source** of year-round interest, because it will attract a variety of birds to your garden in every season.

A birdbath in a strategic spot is a great garden ornament that will bring the magic of birds to any garden. Bright white birdbaths stand out, demanding immediate attention. Darker colors are more subtle; they draw the eye more gently, without being so much of a feature in their own right.

Place outdoor art and other garden structures in a prominent place. A garden statue at the back of a perennial garden draws you to look across all the layers of the garden. Or try yard art in sitting areas, or at the junction of two walks, or in a niche beside a wall.

When using a garden statue in the perennial garden, be sure to select a statue that's tall enough to rise above the perennials (which can hide the base), or set it on blocks or an upside-down pot to give it some extra height.

▲ **A sundial** is a classic garden ornament and seems particularly appropriate for a four-season garden, marking the hours throughout the year.

◄ **Birdhouses serve a practical purpose** in your garden – attracting birds that may help control insect pests – but they also add an artistic or whimsical touch .

5 MORE FOUR-SEASON INTEREST TRICKS Look for ways to add four-season interest in every part of your yard, not just in your perennial garden. Here are some ideas that will boost your yard's looks year-round.

● Set up a trellis between two areas of your yard that you'd like to keep separate. It's a friendly way to separate the children's play area, for example, from a quiet reading area. Plant clematis or another flowering vine to climb the trellis for in-season color, and choose a trellis with a woven lattice or other geometric structure for winter interest.

● Add garden furniture that can withstand the elements through the winter. A classic wooden bench is the ideal accent for a natural garden. Wrought iron furniture fits an old-fashioned garden. For a contemporary garden in mild climates, simple white plastic tables and chairs provide bold relief to a green lawn or shady sitting area.

● Create living lawn art by setting a showy potted tropical plant into a large, attractive container. In the winter, take the plant indoors and fill the container with evergreen branches.

● Highlight the form of a weeping cherry or other decorative tree with garden lights that silhouette the tree at night.

● Put a handsome gazebo near the edge of your property and surround it with perennials. It will be a favorite sitting spot in summer, giving you pleasant memories when you look out from inside your house on a chilly winter day.

Easy-Care Basics

For a great perennial garden, it pays to understand the basic gardening techniques that will help your easy-care perennials get a strong start and live long, healthy lives.

The place to start is your soil. In "Soil Care for Beautiful Perennial Gardens," you'll learn about the different kinds of soil and how they affect plant growth. You'll discover the small miracles that can happen when you add organic matter to your soil. You'll also learn how to make your own compost and use mulch to build your soil's organic matter content.

In "Buying and Planting Perennials," you'll find out where and how to buy quality perennials. There are guidelines for deciding how many perennials to buy when you're planting a garden you've designed yourself. You'll also learn the ins and outs of planting perennials both large and small.

The "Perennial Care Primer" includes how-to instructions for efficient watering. You'll find helpful hints for using soaker hoses and drip irrigation systems. There's plenty of useful information on the best organic fertilizers for perennials. You'll also learn how to stake unobtrusively, revive perennials by dividing, and keep ahead of weeds.

While pests and diseases aren't big problems when you grow easy-care perennials (that's one of the reasons we like them so much!), you can help to discourage any problems by browsing through the tips and techniques covered in the "Perennial Problem Solver." You'll also find helpful hints for preventing deer and other animal pests from feeding on your perennials.

SOIL CARE
FOR BEAUTIFUL
PERENNIAL GARDENS

Great soil care is the true secret of easy-care perennial gardening. After all, the soil is the source of moisture and nutrients your plants need to thrive. And the soil protects the roots and crowns of your perennials. The best time for improving your soil is in the fall. The weather is pleasant, and it's generally a less busy gardening season than spring. So take time to add amendments and work the soil on sunny September and October afternoons. Your fall labors will pay great spring dividends—loose, rich soil ready for planting all your wonderful new perennials.

LEARN ABOUT YOUR SOIL

The first question to answer about your soil is: What kind of soil do you have? There are three basic types of soil: sandy, clay, and loamy. To identify your soil's type, stick your hand in the soil and rub some of it between your fingers.

If it feels gritty and loose, it's sandy soil. Sandy soils are usually well drained and well aerated. (Having air in the soil is important because roots, earthworms, and other soil organisms need air to survive.)

If your soil feels smooth and greasy, it contains lots of clay. You may already know the drawbacks of clay soil. It stays cold and wet in the spring, delaying planting time for perennials. It's also dense and poorly aerated, so plants may grow more slowly.

If your soil crumbles easily between your fingers and is neither gritty nor smooth, it contains moderate amounts of both sand and clay. This type of soil is called loam. Loam is well aerated and holds moisture well. If you have loam soil, count yourself lucky—your perennials will thrive in it.

You can also grow perennials successfully in sandy or clay soils, as long as you improve them before you plant.

Checking Drainage

Soil drainage is the capacity for water to move through the soil. You can't grow easy-care perennials in soggy soil—their roots don't like such wet conditions. Try a simple juice can test to check how well your soil drains. First, remove the top and bottom from a 48-ounce juice can. Dig a shallow, firm-bottomed hole in the soil where you plan to plant your garden. Slip the can into the hole, and fill the can with water.

After an hour goes by, check the water level in the can. If it has dropped 2 to 4 inches, your soil drainage is fine. But if it has dropped less than 2 inches, you need to improve the drainage. (See "Four Fixes for Poorly Drained Soil" on page 73.) Soil that drains faster than 4 inches per hour may be too dry for most perennials. Adding organic matter such as compost or shredded leaves will help the soil retain water longer. (See "Recipes for Soil Improvement" on page 76.)

Checking Soil pH

Soil pH is a measure of the acidity or alkalinity of the soil. It's expressed as a number from 0 to 14 (0 is very acid; 14 is

Sandy soil

Loam soil

Clay soil

very alkaline). The magic numbers for growing most perennials are from 6.0 up to 7.0 (slightly acid to neutral). Some woodland perennials prefer a more acid soil, about 5.5 to 6.5.

It's always a good idea to check pH before you plant perennials. You can pick up a test kit at your local garden center. Many test kits include a special paper that changes color when you press it against some moist soil. Each color matches a certain pH value on a pH color chart in the kit. Just follow the instructions in the kit. If the pH is close to the ideal range, adding organic matter should nudge it into the proper range. That's because organic matter brings both acid and alkaline soils closer to neutral. If your soil is very acidic or alkaline, you'll have to take special steps to change the pH. Ask your Cooperative Extension Service or local nursery owner to explain how to change your soil's pH.

Testing Your Soil

To start a perennial garden with confidence on a brand-new site, have your soil tested before you prepare the bed. A soil test by a professional soil-testing laboratory will give you precise information on soil type and fertility. To find out how to get your soil tested, contact your local extension agent, listed under county or federal offices in the phone book. Many state extension offices have soil-testing programs; others can refer you to a reputable private lab.

Matching Perennials to Your Soil

Some perennials need a rich diet, while others prefer lean conditions. For example, many silver-leaved perennials do best in sandy soils, but most woodland flowers need plenty of moisture and nutrients. (For a detailed list, see "Perennial Soil

---

FOUR FIXES FOR POORLY DRAINED SOIL

If your soil needs better drainage, try one of these techniques.

● Add soil to raise the planting beds 8 inches above ground level. If your natural soil is dense and heavy, combine generous amounts of compost or shredded leaves with the soil you use to build up the beds.

● Be sure downspouts carry rainwater away from the house and garden. Wet soil in beds near your house may be due to overflowing gutters or a plumbing leak. Clean out clogged gutters and repair leaky pipes or faucets.

● Install underground drainage pipes or a small drainage ditch to channel water to a storm sewer or drainage area.

● Eliminate hidden layers of compacted soil that prevent water from soaking deep into the soil. Dig deep to find the compacted soil, then break it up with a shovel or garden fork. Work in compost, aged manure, or shredded leaves to prevent the soil from hardening up again. (When you refill the area where you dug, be sure to put the good topsoil on the surface.)

Preferences" on page 75.) Only the toughest perennials, such as daylilies, tolerate very heavy clay soils. But if you add organic matter to clay soil, you can produce a wonderful site for many perennials, including Siberian iris (*Iris sibirica*), Japanese anemone (*Anemone* x *hybrida*), and astilbes.

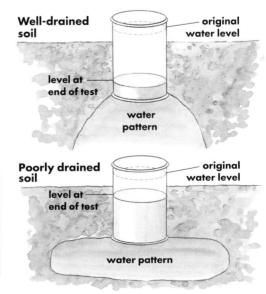

◀ **A simple test** using a bottomless tin can shows how well water moves through soil. In well-drained soil, water moves downward easily; in poorly drained soil, it cannot.

▶ **To make growing perennials** even easier, match your plant combinations to your soil conditions. For example, peonies and Siberian irises both thrive in well-drained, moderately fertile soil.

For an extra-easy perennial garden, choose perennials that grow well in the type of soil you have. When you do, there's little work required to prepare the soil before planting. But if you have favorite perennials that aren't suited to your soil, you can amend your soil to suit the plants or make raised (or sunken) beds. Amending the soil before planting is like scraping and priming a wall before painting. It takes some time and effort, but it ensures great, long-lasting results.

▶ **Fall is the best time** to add organic matter such as decayed leaves to your soil. A rotary tiller speeds up the work when you're starting new beds and borders.

IMPROVE YOUR SOIL

You can improve any kind of soil by adding organic matter—compost, rotted manure, decayed or shredded leaves, straw, grass clippings, and other yard wastes. Organic matter is the great garden equalizer. It makes lean, dry soils more moist and fertile. It helps open up dense clay soils so that plant roots can penetrate and absorb water and nutrients. Organic matter also releases many nutrients, so it's a really effective natural fertilizer.

The best time to improve the soil is in the fall, before you plant perennials. Once the plants are in place, it's much harder to dig and add amendments.

One precaution: If you plan to turn part of your lawn into a garden, don't just dig or till the sod into the soil below. You'll end up with terrible weed problems. Instead, strip off the sod and compost it. Or kill the sod by covering it with a heavy layer of newspaper topped with plastic for up to two months. Once you're sure that all of the weeds and grasses growing in the sod are dead, it's okay to turn under the sod into the soil lying below.

PERENNIAL SOIL PREFERENCES

Many perennials can adapt and grow well in less than optimum conditions. But for the healthiest plants, choose perennials that are suited to your soil and site conditions. Here's a rundown of the soil preferences of the easy-care perennials featured in Part 3 of this book.

Light, Lean, Sandy Soil

Adam's-needle (*Yucca filamentosa*)

Artemisias (*Artemisia* spp.)

Coreopsis (*Coreopsis* spp.)

Garden sage (*Salvia officinalis*)

Lavender (*Lavandula angustifolia*)

Russian sage (*Perovskia atriplicifolia*)

Sea-pink (*Armeria maritima*)

Light, Moderately Fertile Soil

Crocuses (*Crocus* spp.)

Daffodils (*Narcissus* spp.)

Grape hyacinths (*Muscari* spp.)

Grecian windflower (*Anemone blanda*)

Moss phlox (*Phlox subulata*)

Pasque flower (*Anemone pulsatilla*)

Squills (*Scilla* spp.)

Verbenas (*Verbena* spp.)

Yarrows (*Achillea* spp.)

Well-Drained, Moderately Fertile Soil

Alliums (*Allium* spp.)

Balloon flower (*Platycodon grandiflorus*)

Black-eyed Susans (*Rudbeckia* spp.)

Blue false indigo (*Baptisia australis*)

Bugleweeds (*Ajuga* spp.)

Butterfly weed (*Asclepias tuberosa*)

Colewort (*Crambe cordifolia*)

Cranesbills (*Geranium* spp.)

Crocosmias (*Crocosmia* spp.)

Daylilies (*Hemerocallis* spp.)

Early phlox (*Phlox maculata*)

Feather reed grass (*Calamagrostis* × *acutiflora*)

Frikart's aster (*Aster* × *frikartii*)

Garden phlox (*Phlox paniculata*)

Gayfeathers (*Liatris* spp.)

Japanese silver grass (*Miscanthus sinensis*)

Lily-of-the-valley (*Convallaria majalis*)

Peonies (*Paeonia* spp.)

Pincushion flower (*Scabiosa caucasica*)

Purple coneflower (*Echinacea purpurea*)

Sedums (*Sedum* spp.)

Siberian iris (*Iris sibirica*)

Stokes' aster (*Stokesia laevis*)

Tulips (*Tulipa* spp.)

Violet sage (*Salvia* × *superba*)

Virginia bluebells (*Mertensia virginica*)

Winter aconite (*Eranthis hyemalis*)

Yellow corydalis (*Corydalis lutea*)

Moist, Moderately Fertile Soil

Asters (*Aster* spp.)

Bleeding hearts (*Dicentra* spp.)

Bloodroot (*Sanguinaria canadensis*)

Coral bells (*Heuchera* spp.)

Epimediums (*Epimedium* spp.)

Foamflowers (*Tiarella* spp.)

Hellebores (*Helleborus* spp.)

Joe-Pye weed (*Eupatorium fistulosum*)

Lungworts (*Pulmonaria* spp.)

Mints (*Mentha* spp.)

Solomon's seals (*Polygonatum* spp.)

Violets (*Viola* spp.)

Moist, Highly Fertile Soil

Anemones (*Anemone* spp.)

Astilbes (*Astilbe* spp.)

Black snakeroot (*Cimicifuga racemosa*)

Cinnamon fern (*Osmunda cinnamomea*)

Creeping phlox (*Phlox stolonifera*)

Goat's beard (*Aruncus dioicus*)

Hostas (*Hosta* spp.)

Lady ferns (*Athyrium* spp.)

Lady's-mantle (*Alchemilla mollis*)

Siberian bugloss (*Brunnera macrophylla*)

Wild blue phlox (*Phlox divaricata*)

Wild gingers (*Asarum* spp.)

Recipes for Soil Improvement

The following recipes will help you prepare an ideal soil. Before planting, work the amendments into the top 8 to 12 inches of the soil.

MOIST, RICH SOIL

● For heavy clay soil, add a 3-inch layer of coarse sand plus 3 inches of organic matter—compost, decayed leaves, or well-rotted manure—before planting. Every following year, add an inch or two of organic matter as mulch or soil amendment.

● Enrich loam with 3 inches of organic matter when you first prepare the bed. Every year thereafter, add 1 inch of organic matter as mulch or soil amendment.

● Improve light, sandy soils by adding 5 inches of organic matter when you first prepare the bed. Every year after that, add another 3 inches of organic matter as mulch or soil amendment.

LEAN, LIGHT SOIL

● Lighten moderately loamy soils with a 3-inch layer of coarse sand and 2 inches of organic matter when initially preparing the bed. Every following year, add an inch of compost and, for extra-light soil, a coarse sand mulch.

● Keep already-light soils productive by adding an inch or two of organic matter before planting and every year thereafter.

● Don't try to transform heavy clay soil into light soil with amendments. Instead, loosen the soil with a digging fork, then build a light-soil bed on top of it. Create the light soil by mixing 60 percent coarse sand, 35 percent topsoil, and 5 percent organic matter.

Making Compost

Compost is a perennial gardener's all-purpose treasure. Compost happens when you pile together yard wastes, shredded leaves, and vegetable scraps and let them decompose. It's a simple process. The end result is dark, crumbly organic matter that will improve your soil, make an excellent mulch, and feed your perennials.

COMPOST INGREDIENTS

Be inventive in finding local sources of compost materials. A mix of dry, brown and moist, green materials gives the best results. Good ingredients include old straw, leaves (shredded are best), wood chips, pulled weeds (without seeds), grass clippings, spent vegetable plants (such as lettuce or spinach), manure, and kitchen scraps.

If you need more materials than you can find in your own yard, offer to take extra leaves and grass clippings from neighbors. Ask tree-care companies for free wood chips. If you're using large amounts of wood chips, be sure to balance them with some green, nitrogen-rich materials, or decay will be very slow. (You may even want to buy alfalfa pellets to mix in as a nitrogen source.)

There are some materials you *shouldn't* put in your compost pile: weeds that have gone to seed, diseased plants, insect-infested plants, cat and dog droppings, meats, and oils.

COOK UP A BATCH OF FAST COMPOST

Garden centers and mail-order garden suppliers sell attractive plastic and wooden

▼ **A compost pile in the making** shows clear layers of manure, straw, grass clippings, and garden waste. This well-balanced mixture of dry and moist materials will make excellent compost.

bins that keep a compost pile well hidden, so you don't have to worry that your compost will offend your neighbors or detract from the beauty of your perennial gardens. You can also make a compost heap in a simple bin made of wire mesh or slatted boards, or you can simply build a freestanding pile. Follow these easy steps:

1 Gather your dry brown and fresh green materials at your composting site.
2 Spread a 3-foot-square layer of dry materials in your bin or on the spot you've picked for a freestanding pile.
3 Wedge a heavy cardboard tube (like a mailing tube) into the center.
4 Pile up more materials around the tube, mixing dry and moist materials as you go. Add a few handfuls of good garden soil into the mix as you go. (The soil contains the microorganisms that power the decay process.)
5 Over the next few weeks, continue adding materials to the pile until it is 3 feet high. Then stop adding to it and remove the tube to channel air deep into the pile.
6 Mix the materials in the pile with a garden fork every three weeks to encourage fast decay. When the compost is brown and crumbly, it's ready to use.

You can also buy a commercial quick composter. These barrels or bins make turning the pile quick and easy. Simply follow the instructions that come with the composter.

SIMMER A BATCH OF SLOW COMPOST
Making slow compost is a long-term, low-effort project. Build your pile as described previously (at least 3 feet tall, wide, and deep). Then just let it sit – no turning required! After a couple of years, the pile will decompose, forming compost. Because a slow-compost pile is a long-term

▲ **Mulch your perennials** with bark chips or other organic mulch to protect the soil and discourage weeds.

project, you'll probably want to build one in a discreet corner or utility area in your yard.

MULCH TO PROTECT YOUR SOIL
Mulch is the finishing touch for an easy-care perennial garden. A layer of organic material buffers the soil (and the living organisms in it, including plant roots) from abrupt changes in temperature. As it breaks down, your perennials get a steady supply of nutrients. Organic mulches reduce evaporation from the soil, so you won't have to water as often. And mulches discourage weed-seed germination if applied thickly enough.

A MULCH MENU
Choose mulches that are readily available in your area and look good with your plants. This table tells you how deep to spread each type of mulch, as well as some pros and cons.

Mulch	Thickness	Notes
Bark chips	1"–2"	Add nitrogen if necessary.
Coarse sand	1"–2"	Easy to weed.
Cocoa shells	1"–2"	May attract rodents.
Compost	1"–2"	Improves soil, too.
Shredded leaves	3"	Precomposted is best.

BUYING AND PLANTING PERENNIALS

BUYING PLANTS

Whether you stroll through aisles of green plants at a local nursery or page through the tempting descriptions and photos in mail-order catalogs, you're sure to enjoy the beauty and variety of perennials while you shop. But on the practical level, there are two important decisions to make before you buy. How do you want to buy your plants—bareroot, potted, or field-grown? How many plants should you buy? To answer these questions, you'll need to weigh how much you're willing to spend against your wish to have a colorful, well-filled garden quickly.

▼ **The advantage** of buying plants at a nursery is that you can judge the appearance and health of the plants at first hand.

Perennials come in a wide range of prices. You may buy small bareroot plants to get more perennials for your money or choose field-grown plants for convenience and quick bloom. For perennials that grow from bulbs, like daffodils and tulips, the best choice is to buy and plant dormant bulbs. Whatever you choose, treat the plants carefully, and plant them as soon as possible after you buy.

Bareroot Perennials

Many mail-order companies sell bareroot perennials. These plants are generally available only in spring and fall. If you've

never seen bareroot perennials before, their roots' appearance may surprise you. Some have a long taproot like a carrot, others are octopus-like, and still others look like thick mops. These plants are dormant, but they need immediate attention.

Open packages of plants as soon as they arrive, and make sure the roots are moist. If they've dried out, put them in a bucket of lukewarm water for an hour to try to revive them, then wrap them in moist packing material or newspaper until you can get them in the ground. Plan to plant them the same day if possible. (This will be easy if you prepared the bed in early fall.) If you can't plant immediately, store the roots in a cool place for several days. Or plant them in pots and let them grow awhile before planting in the garden.

It's not uncommon for some bareroot perennials to die after planting. Minimize your losses by starting with healthy perennials from reputable nurseries. Some companies guarantee that bareroot perennials will grow and will send replacements for plants that die.

Potted Perennials

Potted perennials offer an easier but often more expensive start for your garden. They come with a full set of active roots and topgrowth, so they withstand transplanting well. You can plant large potted perennials through most of the growing season, except during hot, dry spells, as long as you water them when dry. Plant at least six weeks before frost arrives. It's best to plant small potted perennials (in 3- or 4-inch pots, for example) during moist, cool weather – spring or late summer in cool climates or late fall or winter in warm climates.

Field-Grown Perennials

For field-grown perennials, check at small or specialty growers or in a friend's backyard. Field-grown plants have survived outdoor temperatures—winter cold and summer heat—which proves their hardiness in your climate. Field-grown perennials can be large. Be prepared when you buy them: Bring a large tub, basket, or plastic bag to put your plants in, plus some burlap or newspaper. Keep the roots as intact as possible. Dampen the burlap or newspaper and spread it over the rootballs to keep them moist until planting. Don't delay replanting field-grown perennials; they'll lose vigor quickly while they're out of the ground.

Bulbs

Bulbs are easy to buy in bulk at nursery and garden centers. If you want specific cultivars, though, you may need to order bulbs from mail-order suppliers. Be sure to select firm, heavy bulbs. Buy the biggest bulbs you can afford—they will produce the showiest flowers.

How Many Perennials Should You Buy?

The planting plans in Part 1, beginning on page 8, include recommendations of how many plants you'll need to buy to create the gardens shown. If you follow the plans

---

WILD-COLLECTED PLANTS

Be cautious when buying wildflowers, ferns, and species bulbs. Some nurseries harvest these plants from the wild. Collecting wild plants weakens the native populations; species can become endangered because of wild collecting. Also, the plants harvested may not grow well when transplanted, so wild collecting is bad both for gardeners and the environment. Be sure to buy *nursery-propagated* plants; the phrase "nursery-grown" may be used for plants collected from the wild and then grown for a season at the nursery.

exactly and use the number of plants recommended, your gardens will look full and finished in the first or second season.

If you alter a plan, you'll need to figure out for yourself how many plants to buy. You can judge how far apart to space plants by studying the planting plans. But do give perennials enough room to reach their full size without being overcrowded.

For most perennials, there's a range of possible spacings. Here are two examples: You can plant a large, spreading perennial like Joe-Pye weed (*Eupatorium fistulosum*) from 18 to 24 inches apart. For a smaller, clumping plant like sea-pink (*Armeria maritima*), 8 to 10 inches apart is usual.

You may want to space your perennials a little farther apart than shown in the planting plans. This can save you some money, since you won't need to buy as many plants. Your garden may look a little sparse for the first couple of seasons, but you can plant annuals to fill the gaps.

▼ **Fill gaps** in a new perennial planting by adding annual bedding plants in the spaces between perennials.

STEP-BY-STEP PLANTING TECHNIQUE

Planting perennials in well-prepared soil is easy. If you haven't prepared your soil yet, refer to "Soil Care for Beautiful Perennial Gardens," beginning on page 72.

Planting Bareroot Perennials

Bareroot perennials look small and forlorn when you first plant them. Don't worry! With proper care, they'll soon send out lush, new growth. Here's how to get bareroot perennials off to a great start:

1 Soak roots in lukewarm water for an hour before planting. Remove damaged roots and lank foliage. Dig a hole large enough to hold the roots without curling or twisting.

2 Make a cone of soil in the center to support the plant's crown and keep it just above soil level. Work the roots gently around the cone. For a taproot plant, dig a long, narrow hole, leaving the crown just above soil level.

3 Fill the hole with soil and tamp it down firmly. Then water thoroughly.

Planting Potted Perennials

With potted perennials, you can test your garden design before you plant. Just set each pot on the spot where you plan to plant it. Then step back and see whether the spacing looks even. Make any adjustments you like, then start the planting process.

1 Turn the pot upside down, supporting the base of the plant with one hand. Tap the sides and base to loosen the rootball,

then slip it out gently. Use your finger to separate tangled roots and loosen matted roots. If the tangles or mattings are severe, use a knife to cut them apart.

2 Dig a hole deep and wide enough to hold the roots. Set the plant in the hole. The junction of the stem and roots should be level with the soil surface. If it's not, remove the plant and add soil.

3 Set the plant inside the hole, then fill the hole with soil, working soil around the loose roots as you go. Water the plant slowly and thoroughly.

Planting Field-Grown Perennials

The planting technique for field-grown perennials is very similar to that of potted perennials. The main difference is that you should try to avoid disturbing the roots and rootball—just set the plant in a hole of the proper size, fill it in, and water.

Follow-Up Care For Perennials

Spread a 3-inch layer of organic mulch around your new perennials. Keep the soil moist until the plants begin to grow strongly.

Planting Bulbs

The best time to plant spring-blooming bulbs is in the fall.

1 Dig a hole four times as deep as the height of the bulbs you're planting. For instance, for a 1-inch-high bulb, dig a hole 4 inches deep. Widen the hole so it can accommodate multiple bulbs without them touching.

2 Settle the bulb or bulbs into the hole, root end down. Fill the hole with soil. You can make a two-tiered planting by setting in large bulbs, filling the hole partway with soil, settling smaller bulbs in place, and then topping off the hole with more soil.

3 Tamp the soil down firmly with a rake, then cover the area planted in bulbs with a 2-inch layer of light organic mulch such as shredded leaves. Mark the edges of the bulb planting so you don't accidentally dig into it when planting your other perennials in spring.

PERENNIAL CARE PRIMER

With a great design, good soil, and proper planting, your easy-care perennial garden will grow beautifully without much extra effort from you. But there are times when you'll need to come to the rescue with basic care like watering, fertilizing, and weeding. And there are a few special techniques that you can use to keep your perennial garden beautiful, neat, and healthy, like staking, deadheading, and dividing. Read on for directions on each technique.

WATERING WISDOM

More isn't always better when it comes to watering. Newly planted perennials and moisture-loving perennials do need regular watering to keep the soil evenly moist. But many other perennials need no extra water in climates with regular rainfall. And perennials that prefer lean, dry soil may need watering only during droughts. (See "Perennial Soil Preferences" on page 75 to learn more about the moisture needs of specific plants.)

When you water established perennials, don't just go over them lightly with the hose. Water deeply. A general rule is that plants need an inch of water each week, from rainfall or watering. (They'll need even more during very hot, dry weather.) For young plants with small or shallow root systems, water more frequently so that the top layer of soil stays moist.

▼ **Newly planted** or moisture-loving perennials need regular, deep watering. A soaker hose snaking between the plants will supply them with water.

The easiest and most effective way to water is with trickle or drip irrigation hoses. Because this type of irrigation releases moisture at ground level, it loses little to evaporation. Unlike overhead sprinkling, trickle irrigation won't wet leaves, which can encourage plant diseases.

You can customize a moderately priced drip or trickle irrigation system for your garden. Run small irrigation tubes to every plant or group of plants, selecting different moisture emitters (devices that release water at a specific rate) to provide more water to thirsty plants and less to plants that prefer drier soil. You can hook the irrigation system up to a timer that will automatically turn the system on and off, even when you aren't home. For details, contact an irrigation supplier or specialty mail-order garden supply company that offers drip or trickle irrigation kits.

An inexpensive alternative is soaker hoses. Snake these between plants in a bed. To water, attach your regular garden hose and set it for a slow flow. Soaker hoses have a few disadvantages. Water tends to seep out more quickly at the end closest to the water supply. Also, soaker hoses can clog or kink, cutting off the flow to some parts of the garden.

FERTILIZING FACTS

Like people, some perennials need more food than others. It's as important to avoid overfertilizing as it is underfertilizing. Slow growth, poor flowering, and discolored foliage are all signs that your perennials need a fertilizer boost. Overgrown, floppy foliage is a sign that a plant is in soil that's too rich for its needs. Perennials that prefer lean soil are more prone to disease problems when they grow in rich soil. For general guidelines on the nutrient needs of the perennials in Part 3 of this book, see "Perennial Soil Preferences" on page 75.

Heavy-feeding perennials, especially mature plants, benefit from regular feeding. Many other perennials grow beautifully without extra nutrients if they're planted in fertile soil and mulched with compost. But in lean soil, be sure to fertilize in spring and again before flowering. For more details on when to fertilize perennials, see "Easy-Care Fertilizing" on page 84.

Using Organic Fertilizers

Use a balanced organic fertilizer for perennials, one with a modest percentage of nitrogen and ample amounts of phosphorus and potassium. You can find organic fertilizer blends at most garden

▼ **No extra feeding** is required for many easy-care perennials, including rudbeckias, verbenas, and crocosmias. Just plant them in fertile soil and mulch with compost.

centers; read the label to make sure the product contains only natural ingredients like alfalfa meal, composted manure, guano, blood meal, bonemeal, fish meal, greensand, kelp, rock phosphate, or soybean meal.

Look for a packaged organic fertilizer labeled 2-4-4 or 4-6-6 (these numbers indicate the percentages of nitrogen, phosphorus, and potassium, respectively, in the product). A balanced fertilizer encourages strong root and flower formation as well as steady growth. Apply fertilizer blends according to the instructions on the package.

Liquid fertilizers such as fish emulsion and compost tea will give your plants a quick boost in growth, but they won't have a long-lasting effect. To brew compost tea, put a shovelful of compost in a burlap bag, and soak it in a 5-gallon bucket full of water for two or three days. Remove the bag (you can put the compost back in your compost pile), and use the liquid to fertilize your garden.

EASY-CARE FERTILIZING

Plan your fertilizing schedule according to the natural needs of your plants.

For perennials that prefer rich soil: When the first shoots emerge in spring, pull back the mulch around the plants, and sprinkle a balanced granular organic blended fertilizer around the edges of the shoots. Use a trowel or hand fork to work it lightly into the soil. Then add a fresh inch or two of finished compost. If growth seems weak in early summer or before bloom, water with compost tea.

For perennials that thrive in lean soil: Add 1 inch of finished compost mulch around the edges of emerging plants in spring. If growth is still slow in early summer, try watering the plants with compost tea.

For spring-flowering bulbs: Side dress with a balanced organic fertilizer blend in early fall. In summer, allow the bulb foliage to yellow before removing it.

Granular and slow-release fertilizers, such as cottonseed meal (which supplies nitrogen), release nutrients gradually over a period of weeks or months. Greensand (a good source of potassium) can work for up to ten years, offering a long-term remedy for a potassium deficiency.

▲ **Remove large weeds** by pulling firmly at the base of the stem. If the weeds don't yield, loosen the roots with a hand fork and pull again.

WIPING OUT WEEDS

Weeding makes your gardens look neat, but more important, it eliminates hiding places for pests and diseases and prevents unwanted plants from crowding out your flowers. Take special care to control weeds in a new garden bed. Weed seeds sprout easily in the newly worked soil and in the open spaces between young perennial plants. When you first prepare a bed, be sure to remove all of the perennial weed roots you find. Try these strategies for controlling weeds in your perennial beds:

● Prevent lawngrass from creeping into perennial beds by installing a sturdy edging strip between the bed and the lawn.

▲ **To keep tough weeds down,** cover the soil with several layers of newspaper topped with organic mulch.

● After planting, cover open areas with several layers of newspaper topped with 2 inches of organic mulch. In hot, dry climates, you can substitute corrugated cardboard for the newspaper.

● In places where you cannot mulch, run a hoe over the soil surface at least once a week during spring and early summer to uproot any weed seedlings that appear. Hand-pull large weeds, tugging gently at the base of the stems to uproot them.

● If a weed is growing snugly against a perennial, cut off the intruder with pruning shears to avoid damaging the perennial.

● For spiny, seedy, or rash-inducing weeds, put a plastic bread bag over your hand and arm, grab the weed, pull the plastic down over the weed, and bag it up. You can throw away the seedy or prickly weeds and reuse the bag, unless the weed in question is poison ivy. In that case, just throw away the weed, bag and all.

STAKING STRATEGIES

Perennials with narrow stems or full, heavy flowers are prone to flopping. Delicate stems may simply bend, but stronger stems may break at the base. Most of the easy-care perennials in this book are self-supporting. The exceptions are tall asters and black-eyed Susans. (Some gardeners like the cascading look of these plants when left to flop, while others want

▼ **Use plant stakes** to keep your perennials from falling flat. Linking plant stakes (*below left*) work well for groups of upright perennials. Hoop supports (*below*) are a good choice for floppy perennials.

► **Dead-heading** with hedge clippers can save time for large clumps of perennials like lady's-mantle or bee balm that hold their flowers above the foliage.

the upright impact of staked plants.) Other perennials will occasionally need staking if you accidentally overfertilize them or if you site sun-loving plants in partial shade.

There are several ways to support floppy perennials. The key is to put the support in place long before a plant falls flat on its face in your garden.

● Let perennials lean on sturdy neighbors such as a shrub, bearded iris, or hosta.
● Pinch back low- to moderate-size bushy perennials, such as coreopsis and 'Autumn Joy' sedum, in midspring. They will branch out, stay compact, and be less likely to flop.
● Set a low, wire-mesh cage over an emerging bushy plant. The stems will grow through the cage. Once the stems fill out, they will hide the wire.
● Train plants that need support at the base through wire hoops or squares of linking stakes.
● Tie perennials with upright flower spikes to individual bamboo stakes that are almost as tall as the mature flower stem. Put the stakes in place in spring. As the flower stems grow, gently tie them to the stakes with strips of panty hose or with soft, green plant ties.

DEADHEADING DETAILS

If you let your perennials set seed, they'll use lots of their energy producing the seed instead of more leaves and flowers. Also, the seeds may scatter around the garden, resulting in hundreds of seedlings that can be as pesky as weeds. To prevent both of these problems, deadhead—remove flowers as they fade, before they set seed.

Deadheading prolongs flowering of many easy-care perennials, including yarrows (*Achillea* spp.), lady's-mantle (*Alchemilla mollis*), sea-pink (*Armeria maritima*), coreopsis, bleeding hearts (*Dicentra eximia*), purple coneflower (*Echinacea purpurea*), 'Stella D'Oro' daylily (*Hemerocallis*), early phlox (*Phlox maculata*), salvias, pincushion flower (*Scabiosa caucasica*), and Stokes' aster (*Stokesia laevis*). When you deadhead, you can cut off the old flowers one by one or remove entire flowering stems after all of the flower buds have opened. But look closely before you cut because some unopened flower buds may be hidden below the faded flowers. If you find some, just snip off the faded blooms above, so you can enjoy the flowers beneath.

Some perennials have such attractive seedpods that you won't want to deadhead them. These include butterfly weed (*Asclepias tuberosa*), astilbes, blue false indigo (*Baptisia australis*), purple coneflower (*Echinacea purpurea*), orange coneflower (*Rudbeckia fulgida*), Lenten rose (*Helleborus orientalis*), and many ornamental grasses.

DIVIDENDS OF DIVIDING

Over the years, many perennials creep outward, overgrowing neighboring plants. Some perennials become hollow in the center as they spread. Bulbs may stop flowering with age. The easy cure to all of these problems is division—the simple process of uprooting a plant and cutting or pulling sections of the roots apart. Replanting the sections in fresh soil rejuvenates the plant as well as the garden.

Bulbs are especially easy to divide. As the foliage yellows, unearth the bulbs and separate the mature mother bulbs from the smaller offspring. Enrich the soil with compost, and replant with the flat end where the roots will grow on the bottom and the pointed shoot end facing up.

You can divide a large perennial clump into three moderate-size clumps that you can replant to create a lovely grouping. Or replant just the best clump and give away the others. If you're expanding your gardens and want lots of new plants to fill them, you can divide the clump into a dozen small sections, each with at least a couple of shoots and roots.

Divide summer- or fall-blooming perennials in spring, as the shoots emerge from the ground. Divide spring-blooming perennials in late summer or early fall. Perennials with many fibrous roots, such as Japanese anemones (*Anemone* x *hybrida*) and bugleweeds (*Ajuga* spp.), are easy to break apart with your hands.

For fleshy-rooted perennials such as daylilies (*Hemerocallis* spp.), dig up the clump, use a hose to wash off the soil, then roll the plant on the ground to loosen the roots. Divide by hand or pry apart with two garden forks inserted back to back into the clump. You may have to use a knife or shovel to separate the roots of older plants.

Not all perennials need dividing. Some, including butterfly weed (*Asclepias tuberosa*) and blue false indigo (*Baptisia australis*), have long taproots that can't be cut apart. Other perennials, such as astilbes, hostas, Siberian iris, and peonies, grow slowly into magnificent mature plants that seldom need to be rejuvenated.

▲ **To divide tough clumps** of perennials or ferns, insert two garden forks back to back, and then push the handles apart.

HEADING OFF PROBLEMS

When you keep up with seasonal chores like watering, fertilizing, and deadheading, your perennials usually grow and bloom without problems. In general, the easy-care perennials recommended in this book aren't prone to pest or disease problems. But if you find signs of insects or disease, look for the solutions in the "Perennial Problem Solver," beginning on page 88, and take prompt action to keep the trouble from spreading any further.

PERENNIAL PROBLEM SOLVER

The easy-care perennials recommended in this book are generally trouble-free. But occasionally they may need a little attention to prevent or control pests or diseases.

PREVENTING DISEASE PROBLEMS

If you've planted your perennials in the right soil and sun or shade conditions, you're off to a good start in preventing disease problems. Choosing disease-resistant or disease-tolerant types and cultivars also helps you sidestep some common diseases of perennials. For instance, early phlox (*Phlox maculata*) is resistant to powdery mildew, a common fungal disease that plagues garden phlox (*P. paniculata*). But if you love garden phlox, try one of the mildew-resistant cultivars like 'David'.

Most disease organisms need moist conditions to thrive. Keeping foliage dry helps reduce disease problems, so use a drip or trickle irrigation setup rather than watering with sprinklers or a handheld hose. Good air circulation also helps because it keeps the air around your plants from becoming too humid.

Despite these precautions, you may find plants in your garden that have blemished or rotted leaves, stems, or roots. When you do, always remove the diseased plant parts, and burn them or put them in a sealed plastic bag to discard with your trash. This helps prevent the problem from spreading. If a severe disease problem strikes your garden, take samples of the diseased plants to your local Cooperative Extension Service for help in identifying the problem. See "Solving Problems" on page 91 for symptoms and controls for common disease problems of perennials.

For some fungal diseases, spraying your plants with a baking soda solution (½ teaspoon in 2 cups of water) or fungicidal soap can keep the infection from spreading. Sulfur or copper sprays are also acceptable for use in organic gardens, and they can help prevent most fungal and bacterial diseases.

PREVENTING AND CONTROLLING PESTS

To control pests (and also diseases), you have to know what you're dealing with. Inspect the plant to find the culprit or samples of the damage it causes. "Solving Problems" on page 91 will help you decide what kind of insect pest or other predator is feasting on your plants. You can also consult "Recommended Reading" on page 155 or contact your local Cooperative Extension Service for help.

Pest Control Tricks

Once you've identified the pest, find out how you can eliminate its hiding places or overwintering haunts. Good garden cleanup practices, like removing and composting the old leaves and stems, may be all it takes. Also, choose a control method that does the least damage to the garden environment. Barriers and traps are a great way to start. If you have to use a spray, use a mild, organic product labeled for that particular pest. Read the product label and follow directions carefully to be sure the results will be safe and effective. Reapply as suggested to kill future generations of pests.

Life Cycle of a Japanese Beetle

In summer and fall, adult beetles feed on garden plants

Beetles lay eggs in late summer

In spring, larvae move up and feed on grass roots

They pupate in early summer

In winter, larvae hide deep in the soil

Larvae hatch and move deeper in the soil

BLOCK PEST PROBLEMS

Just as you'd screen off a porch to escape mosquitoes, you can put up a barricade to keep pests away from your perennials. Barricades are easy to install and surprisingly effective. Here are some to try:

● To prevent cutworm damage, surround newly planted seedlings with cutworm collars. To make the collars, cut cardboard paper towel tubes into 3-inch-long sections. Push 1 inch of the collar into the soil around the seedling. Cutworms can't tunnel through the collar to nip off the stem. Remove the collar as the plant matures.

● Block out slugs and snails by surrounding beds with a copper strip, which will shock the slimy creatures if they try to cross it.

● Plant edible bulbs, such as crocuses and tulips, beneath a cage of ¼-inch hardware cloth to keep out chipmunks, squirrels, and other rodents. Or you can plant bulbs that critters won't eat, such as daffodils (*Narcissus* spp.) and squills (*Scilla* spp.).

SIMPLE TRAPS THAT WORK

You can use simple traps to catch pests. One of the best is a homemade slug trap. Bury a margarine tub so that its rim is at the soil surface, and fill it with beer. The beer attracts slugs, which crawl in and can't get out.

▲ **Learning about** pest life cycles will help you control the pests. For example, Japanese beetles start life as soil-dwelling grubs, and there are effective organic controls for the grubs.

SLUG-PROOF PLANTS

In shady or moist conditions, slugs can chew perennials to ribbons. Some gardeners suggest that slugs aren't fond of the taste of certain perennials, making them the best (and possibly only) plants to try in badly slug-infested spots. Choices include coral bells (*Heuchera* spp.), goat's beard (*Aruncus dioicus*), daffodils (*Narcissus* spp.), and squills (*Scilla* spp.).

◄ **Pour beer** into a shallow container set in your garden to attract and trap slugs.

Use yellow plastic rectangles coated with sticky Tanglefoot or Vaseline to catch aphids and whiteflies. These sticky traps will also attract beneficial insects, so only put them in your garden when you know you have a problem with one of these pests.

ATTRACT BENEFICIAL INSECTS AND PARASITES

When you garden organically, you'll attract powerful problem preventers—beneficial insects. Ladybugs, lacewings, spiders, and other insect predators eat plant-eating pests. Tiny trichogramma wasps and other beneficial parasites lay their eggs in the bodies of pest insects. After they hatch, the larvae eat the pests from the inside.

Populations of beneficials will increase when you plant a variety of flowers for alternative food sources and put out very shallow containers of water so that the insects can drink without drowning. Most important, to encourage beneficials, don't use insecticides. You also can order some types of beneficial insects from mail-order suppliers and release them in your garden.

Parasitic nematodes are microscopic, wormlike creatures that feed on pests that spend part of their life cycle in the soil, such as Japanese beetle grubs. You can buy packets of parasitic nematodes from mail-order suppliers to add to your soil. Follow the instructions on the package carefully when applying the nematodes. One unusual control method for Japanese beetles actually uses bacteria to kill the pest. Milky disease spores are spores of bacteria that infect Japanese beetle grubs. Spread it on your lawn (which is where the grubs feed) to reduce the population of Japanese beetles that will trouble your perennial garden.

USE SOAP AND OIL SPRAYS

Spraying your perennials with insecticidal soap will kill soft-bodied insects. Soaps are nontoxic to animals and most beneficial insects but control aphids, whiteflies, leafhoppers, spider mites, and other pests. Spray according to product instructions.

A gentle coating of highly refined horticultural oil (called summer oil) can smother pests such as scale and aphids. Be sure you buy summer or superior oil, and follow the product instructions carefully when you apply it. Don't use dormant oil, which can damage tender leaves and stems.

DEALING WITH DEER AND OTHER ANIMAL PESTS

For deer, you'll need to erect a fence 8 to 12 feet high. A lower fence may work if you install a single strand of 30-inch-high, battery-powered electric wire fence 3 feet outside of the garden fence.

To increase the effectiveness of an electric fence, put aluminum foil flags coated with peanut butter on the wire (disconnect the power source first). The deer lick the peanut butter, get a shock, and quickly learn to avoid the fence. An odor barrier, such as coyote urine, may also keep animals out if you reapply it frequently around the perimeter of your yard or garden. For a commercial supplier of these products, refer to "Sources," on page 155.

Other odor barriers, such as dried blood and cayenne pepper sprinkled around plants, should be fairly effective for keeping rabbits, groundhogs, and other animals from munching your perennials.

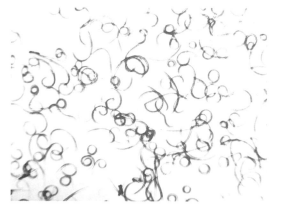

▼ **Parasitic nematodes** (magnified here) are great for quick control of many common insect pests.

SOLVING PROBLEMS

Check this chart to identify and control the most common pest and disease problems in the perennial garden.

PESTS

Symptom	Pest Description	Pest Name	Control	
Leaves with large holes	Glossy, metallic beetle	Japanese beetle	Apply commercial product containing milky disease spores or parasitic nematodes.	Japanese beetles
Leaves with large, ragged holes; slime trails on leaves	Soft-bodied gray, black, or brown creatures with or without a hard shell	Slug or snail	Set out beer traps; install copper strip around garden.	Slug
Distorted shoots and leaves; sticky, sometimes black-coated stems and leaves	Tiny, soft-bodied, pear-shaped insects	Aphids	Set out sticky yellow traps; encourage beneficial insects; spray with insecticidal soap.	
Brown tunnels in leaves	Pale green maggots, not visible on outside of leaf	Leafminers	Remove and destroy infested leaves.	Aphids
Discolored, speckled leaves	Specks on webbing on underside of leaves	Spider mites	Keep plants well watered; spray with insecticidal soap.	
Sticky, distorted growth	White cottony tufts that flutter up when disturbed	Whiteflies	Encourage beneficial insects; spray with insecticidal soap.	Leafminer damage

DISEASES

Symptom	Disease	Control
Blackened, curling flowers on peony buds; brown leaf spots	Botrytis blight	Remove and destroy infected plants; thin plants to improve air circulation.
Rusty spots on underside of leaves	Rust	Remove and destroy infected plants; apply sulfur dust to prevent spread.
White coating on new leaves during hot, humid days	Powdery mildew	Plant resistant cultivars; apply a baking soda spray; if problems have been severe in the past, apply sulfur spray.
Wilting leaves and stems; rotten roots or crown	Root and crown rots	Remove and destroy infected plant parts; replant in soil with better drainage.

Easy-Care
Perennial
Encyclopedia

Once you've decided which of the easy-care gardens from "Easy-Care Garden Designs" you want to plant, and boned up on the perennial gardening techniques covered in "Easy-Care Basics," you'll want more details on the specific perennials you plan to try. The following rundown of 60 easy-care perennials will supply all the information you need to grow and use these terrific plants in your garden.

Plant Names

To find plants in this "Easy-Care Perennial Encyclopedia," look for them alphabetically by botanical name. Botanical names include genus and species names. For example, the botanical name for garden peony is *Paeonia officinalis*. It's a good idea to become familiar with botanical names of perennials, because they're often listed that way in mail-order catalogs. Of course, each entry also lists the most familiar common names for each perennial. So if you don't know the botanical name of a particular plant, look up its common name in the index to find the page listing for the plant.

Appearance

Each plant entry includes descriptions of the perennial, including the best cultivars. Cultivars are special variations developed by plant breeders; a cultivar has particular characteristics like flower color, size, and disease resistance that make it desirable. You'll find all the cultivars used in the garden designs in "Easy-Care Garden Designs," and more besides.

Garden Uses

In this section of each entry, I've suggested groups of perennials that look good and grow well together, so you can dabble in creating your own designs.

Growing and Propagation

In this section, you'll find tips on planting and caring for each perennial that will help you keep it in top form. I've also given instructions on when and how to propagate to increase your supply of plants.

Baptisia 107

Baptisia australis
BLUE FALSE INDIGO

Add height and interesting texture to perennial beds with the cloverlike leaves and striking blue flowers of blue false indigo.

Blue false indigo flowers add valuable early-summer color to a bed or border, but the blue-green foliage is an asset too.

APPEARANCE Blue false indigo has spikes of bright blue flowers that rise from 2 to 4 feet tall. The blue-green leaves, which resemble clover, were once fermented to produce a blue dye. The dark seedpods remain interesting long after the flowers have faded.

GARDEN USES Use blue false indigo in the middle or rear of a flower garden. The cool blue flowers are a perfect complement to pink peonies, bleeding hearts (*Dicentra* spp.), and cranesbills (*Geranium* spp.). They contrast nicely with silver artemisia foliage

or with golden and orange flowers, such as fernleaf yarrow (*Achillea millefolium*).

GROWING AND PROPAGATION Plant in sun or light shade and fertile, moist but well-drained soil. In shady sites, let the plant grow up through a supporting ring or grid. Deadhead to encourage long bloom or allow the seedpods to form for summer and fall interest. This is one perennial that stays put in the garden and won't require division. To increase your supply of plants, take cuttings from the tips of stems after flowering ends.

Plant Profile

HARDINESS
Zones 3-9

SEASON OF BLOOM
Late spring and early summer

LIGHT REQUIREMENTS

MOISTURE REQUIREMENTS

HEIGHT
2 - 4 feet

SPREAD
3 - 4 feet

How to Use the Plant Profiles

For quick details such as season of bloom, moisture requirements, and height,
check the "Plant Profile" feature in each plant entry. Here's what you'll find.

1 Hardiness

Hardiness refers to how much winter cold a perennial can tolerate. The United States is divided into climatic zones based on average minimum temperatures, as shown in the map on page 154. Climatic zones with higher numbers are warmer in winter (and usually in summer too) and zones with lower numbers are colder. For example, a perennial hardy in Zone 4 can withstand winter temperatures of about 20°F.

Recent research has shown that summer heat also influences perennial survival. Many perennials require a cold winter rest period, which limits their range to Zones 8 or 9 in the South. Perennials such as pincushion flower (*Scabiosa caucasica*) thrive in cool climates but suffer in blazing heat, especially when combined with humidity. Because of this, pincushion flower usually doesn't grow well south of Zone 7.

Consider hardiness zones as a guideline, rather than a hard-and-fast rule. You may want to experiment with a less-than-hardy plant by planting it in well-drained soil and a warm location near your house. But for a truly easy-care perennial garden, it's wise to stick with plants that are reliable in your local area. That means selecting species that are completely heat- *and* cold-hardy and won't need special care to thrive.

2 Season of Bloom

This covers the range of times when species of a given perennial may be in bloom. For example, the phlox entry lists bloom times of spring and summer. This reflects the fact that there are spring-blooming phloxes like creeping phlox, and summer bloomers like garden phlox. Check the descriptions in the entry for details on when a particular species of perennial blooms.

3 Light Requirements

Sunlight is another critical factor that influences how well perennials perform. Some perennials require full sun – 6 hours or more of direct sunlight each day. In the Plant

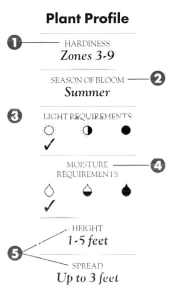

Plant Profile

① — HARDINESS
Zones 3-9

SEASON OF BLOOM — **②**
Summer

③ LIGHT REQUIREMENTS
☼ ◑ ●
✓

MOISTURE — **④**
REQUIREMENTS
◌ ◖ ●
✓

HEIGHT
1-5 feet

⑤
SPREAD
Up to 3 feet

Profiles, these perennials have a check below the unshaded sun symbol. If your yard is in light shade and only receives 4 to 6 hours of sun a day, it's best not to attempt to grow sun-loving perennials. You'll have plenty of great choices among perennials that thrive in partial shade (indicated by a check below the half-darkened sun). For plants that do well in full shade or less than 4 hours of sun a day, look for a check below the fully darkened sun.

☼ ◑ ●
full sun   **partial shade**   **full shade**

4 Moisture Requirements

The water droplet symbol in the Plant Profiles indicates moisture requirements. Moisture levels tend to be higher in clay soil and soils rich in organic matter; they're also higher in climates with abundant rainfall. Drier soils tend to occur in sandy areas or dry climates. Plants such as lavender that require soil that is on the dry side have a check below the unfilled water droplet. For evenly moist soil, look for perennials marked with a check below the half-filled droplet. Plants that need constantly moist soils are noted by a check below the filled-in droplet.

◌ ◖ ●
low moisture   **moderate moisture**   **high moisture**

5 Height and Spread

Use the height and spread information in the Plant Profiles to help you plan your own garden. Set tall plants back far enough in the garden so they won't block your view of shorter plants. When you plant new gardens, or slip a perennial into an opening in an existing garden, give the plants enough room to fill out to their mature spread. This prevents overcrowding and helps keep perennials healthy.

Armed with all this great information, you'll be well prepared for planting and enjoying your easy-care perennial garden. You'll be rewarded for your efforts with a garden full of beautiful flowers for years to come.

Achillea spp.

YARROW

*Add a feathery touch to a sunny garden with
yarrow's ferny foliage and abundant,
long-lasting flowers.*

'Coronation Gold' yarrow adds vibrant yellow flowers to a mixed border throughout the summer.

Plant Profile

HARDINESS
Zones 3-9

SEASON OF BLOOM
Summer

LIGHT REQUIREMENTS
☼   ◐   ●
✓

MOISTURE REQUIREMENTS
💧   💧   💧
✓

HEIGHT
1-5 feet

SPREAD
Up to 3 feet

APPEARANCE Yarrows have finely cut leaves that spread in feathery mats near the ground. Most have large flat-topped clusters of small yellow, white, pink, or red flowers.

'Moonshine', a hybrid yarrow (Zones 3 to 8), grows up to 2 feet tall with soft yellow flowers and gray-tinted foliage. It does best in climates without high humidity in summer.

Fernleaf yarrow (*A. filipendulina*) is a bold, golden-flowered yarrow that reaches 3 to 5 feet tall. The more compact 'Cloth of Gold' grows 2 to 4 feet tall. Sturdy 'Parker's Variety' reaches 3 to 4 feet and seldom needs staking.

The hybrid 'Coronation Gold' grows to 3 feet tall, has gray-tinted foliage, and produces golden flowers for up to 3 months. It grows well in areas with high summer humidity.

Common yarrow (*A. millefolium*) has handsome pink, red, or white flowers on branching stems that may need staking for support. Hybrid cultivars include red 'Paprika' and pastel pink 'Apple Blossom'. Woolly yarrow (*A. tomentosa*; Zones 3 to 7) forms a mat of furry gray foliage with golden flowers to 9 inches tall.

GARDEN USES Use woolly yarrow to edge an herb or perennial garden. Taller yarrows are great for the middle or rear of a flower border or island bed. Try combining 'Coronation Gold' yarrow with violet sage (*Salvia* x *superba*) and porcupine grass (*Miscanthus sinensis* var. *strictus*).

GROWING AND PROPAGATION Plant yarrow in full sun and light, well-drained soil of moderate fertility. The stems may need support to stay upright. Once established, yarrow is drought-tolerant. Avoid fertilizing except in very poor soils. Divide every 3 years, or as needed to encourage blooming and prevent excessive spread. Remove faded flowers, cutting back to new flower buds. Remove spent flower stems at their base to keep the plant tidy and prevent self-sowing.

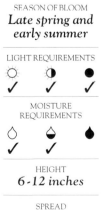

Ajuga spp.
BUGLEWEED, AJUGA

*Carpet a bed or a lawn with bugleweed's
clear blue flower spikes and neat
ground-hugging foliage.*

APPEARANCE Bugleweeds are creeping groundcovers that grow into mats of handsome rounded leaves punctuated in spring by abundant spikes of small tubular blossoms.

Blue-flowered Geneva bugleweed (*A. genevensis*; Zones 4 to 9) reaches 6 to 12 inches tall in bloom; it may also have pink or white flowers.

Upright bugleweed (*A. pyramidalis*) stays lower, about 9 inches tall when covered with blue flower spikes. 'Metallica Crispa' has wavy, crinkled purple leaves that get darker in the fall.

Common bugleweed (*A. reptans*) is 10 inches tall when in bloom, with flowers of a beautiful clear blue. Several cultivars are more ornamental: 'Atropurpurea' has purple leaves; 'Burgundy Glow' foliage is a rainbow of white, pink, and green; and 'Bronze Beauty' has purple leaves and purple flowers.

GARDEN USES Let bugleweed spread across the foreground of an island bed or form a carpet to edge a flower or shrub garden. 'Burgundy Glow' looks great in light shade combined with pink astilbes and white-edged hostas. Common bugleweed will spread eagerly into adjoining lawns; use a barrier to keep it in place or learn to enjoy its cheerful spring display in your lawngrass.

GROWING AND PROPAGATION
Bugleweeds are carefree, adaptable plants that grow well in sun or shade. They'll spread at a moderate rate in average soil; in rich, loose, moist soil, they'll cover ground rapidly. Remove faded flower spikes to keep the plants tidy. Divide as needed to control size and increase your bugleweed collection. If sections die back, dig them out and throw away the dead plants. Refill the area with fresh soil and replant new starts of bugleweed.

For a stylish groundcover, try 'Catlin's Giant' bugleweed, which develops large leaves and showy blue flower spikes.

Plant Profile

HARDINESS
Zones 3-9

SEASON OF BLOOM
Late spring and early summer

LIGHT REQUIREMENTS

MOISTURE REQUIREMENTS

HEIGHT
6-12 inches

SPREAD
8-10 inches; clumps up to several feet

Alchemilla mollis
LADY'S-MANTLE

Give lady's-mantle a place of honor in the front of the border where its dew-spangled foliage and clouds of airy chartreuse blossoms can be admired.

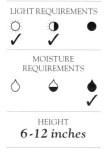

Lady's-mantle forms rounded mounds of foliage topped by yellow-green flowers that make an attractive groundcover.

Plant Profile

HARDINESS
Zones 3-8

SEASON OF BLOOM
Spring and early summer

LIGHT REQUIREMENTS

MOISTURE
REQUIREMENTS

HEIGHT
6-12 inches

SPREAD
1-2 feet

APPEARANCE Short, frothy sprays of chartreuse flowers emerge from a clump of attractive round, pleated leaves. The leaves are lightly covered with hairs that catch morning dew or raindrops and sparkle in the sunlight. The plant forms a neat mound to 12 inches tall.

GARDEN USES The long-lasting flowers and handsome leaves of lady's-mantle are lovely companions for many perennials. Plant groups of three or five in the front or middle of a perennial border. The unusual color of the flowers looks surprisingly pretty paired with blues, purples, and yellows. Try planting lady's-mantle with yellow Siberian iris (*Iris sibirica*) and orange butterfly weed (*Asclepias tuberosa*). It also makes a beautiful edging plant or groundcover for a flower or shrub garden.

GROWING AND PROPAGATION
Lady's-mantle needs moist, rich soil and irrigation during dry weather. If conditions become too dry, the leaf margins will turn brown. Plant in full sun in cool climates or light shade in warm climates. To rejuvenate foliage, cut it back in midsummer and let the leaves resprout. Divide clumps as needed to expand your collection. Remove faded flower stems to keep the plant neat and encourage extended bloom.

Allium spp.
ALLIUM

Add a spark to your perennial garden with the spiky pink flower globes or white starry flower clusters of these sweet-smelling onion relatives.

APPEARANCE These ornamental members of the onion family have globe-shaped clusters of small white, pink, or purple flowers. Although the leaves often carry a hint of onion odor, the flowers are usually sweet smelling. Alliums grow from bulbs that produce slim, linear leaves.

Giant onion (*A. giganteum*; Zones 4 to 8) sends up large, purple flowerheads on bare stems to 5 feet tall.

A. senescens has twisting, 1-foot green or gray foliage that persists through the summer. It bears reddish purple flower clusters up to 30 inches tall. 'Glaucum' has handsome silver leaves to 6 inches tall and pink flowers to 16 inches tall in late summer and fall.

Common chives (*A. schoeno-prasum*) grows in a neat tuft of upright foliage that lasts all season and has pink to purple flowers to 18 inches tall.

Garlic chives (*A. tuberosum*; Zones 4 to 8) has flat, straplike dark green leaves that reach 15 inches long and last all season. The foliage has a mild garlic scent and flavor, while the white flowers, borne in late summer and fall, smell like roses.

GARDEN USES Use tall alliums with leaves that don't go dormant, such as chives, in the middle of a perennial garden. The silver foliage of *A. senescens* 'Glaucum' makes an interesting garden edging. Plant giant

Rounded *Allium senescens* flowers add a splash of late summer color. Deadhead the flowers promptly to prevent self-seeding.

onion and other tall, bare-stemmed alliums between clumps of leafy perennials such as cranesbills (*Geranium* spp.) and lady's-mantle (*Alchemilla mollis*). For a beautiful and aromatic combination, grow chives with lavender and garden sage.

GROWING AND PROPAGATION Alliums grow well in full sun with fertile, well-drained soil. To increase your plants, divide the bulbs or rhizomes as the foliage begins to die back. Some alliums, including chives, will self-sow freely. Making divisions is easier than transplanting seedlings, so deadhead promptly to avoid having to weed out seedlings.

Plant Profile

HARDINESS
Zones 3-9

SEASON OF BLOOM
Spring, summer, and fall

LIGHT REQUIREMENTS
☼ ◑ ●
✓

MOISTURE REQUIREMENTS
◊ ◐ ●
✓

HEIGHT
6 inches - 5 feet

SPREAD
15 inches - 2 feet

Anemone spp.
ANEMONE, WINDFLOWER

*Charming anemone blossoms will add grace to
a woodland wildflower garden or a mixed border
in shade or sun.*

White Japanese anemones like 'Honorine Jobert' are a great choice for mixed borders with rich, well-drained soil.

Plant Profile

HARDINESS
Zones 3-8

SEASON OF BLOOM
Spring, summer, or fall

LIGHT REQUIREMENTS
☼ ◑ ●
✓ ✓

MOISTURE REQUIREMENTS
◌ ◐ ◆
✓ ✓

HEIGHT
6 inches - 5 feet

SPREAD
8 inches - 2 feet

APPEARANCE Anemones have round, open flowers with clusters of golden stamens in the center. Some species are low-growing; others send up tall flower-stalks. The leaves usually are deeply lobed.

Snowdrop anemone (*A. sylvestris*) has white flowers to 18 inches tall in spring and reblooms in fall. The fluffy seedheads can be ornamental too.

Japanese anemone (*A. x hybrida*; Zones 5 to 8) blooms in late summer or fall. It grows 3 to 5 feet tall with pink or white flowers to 4 inches across. Good cultivars include white 'Honorine Jobert'; double-flowered white 'Whirlwind'; compact, double-flowered pink 'Prince Henry'; and pink 'Queen Charlotte'.

Grecian windflower (*A. blanda*; Zones 4 to 8) produces blue, pink, or white flowers to 8 inches tall in spring, then becomes dormant.

Pasque flower (*A. pulsatilla*), another spring bloomer, grows to 10 inches tall with white or purple flowers. It also produces attractive furry buds and leaves and feathery seedheads.

GARDEN USES Scatter groups of Grecian windflower bulbs through any bed for spring color. Use snowdrop anemones and pasque flowers in the front or middle of a flower garden, or let them spread in a woodland garden. Combine them with bloodroot (*Sanguinaria canadensis*) and variegated Solomon's seal (*Polygonatum odoratum* 'Variegatum'). Japanese anemones are nice for the rear of a border. Or put them in masses of five or seven between trees and shrubs.

GROWING AND PROPAGATION Plant Japanese and snowdrop anemones in rich, moist but well-drained soil in sun to light shade. Pasque flower and Grecian windflower form tubers; they need fast-draining soil in light shade (or sun in cool climates). To prevent premature dormancy, irrigate during drought. Divide snowdrop and Japanese anemones as needed to control their spread.

Armeria maritima
SEA-PINK, COMMON THRIFT

The tidy cushions of sea-pink foliage accented by pink flowers lend a formal touch to the edge of a sunny perennial bed.

'Laucheana' sea-pinks make a showy display of bright pink ball shaped flowers and grassy foliage.

APPEARANCE Sea-pink bears neat mounds of evergreen, grasslike foliage. Elegant round clusters of pink or white flowers rise on slim stems to 8 inches tall in late spring and reappear sporadically through the summer if deadheaded regularly. Cultivars offer a variety of colors including white 'Alba', pink 'Vindictive', and red 'Dusseldorf Pride'. 'Robusta' bears pink flowers on stems to 15 inches tall. 'Bees' Ruby' grows to 15 inches tall with red flowers and slightly broader leaves.

GARDEN USES Use sea-pink to edge a flower or shrub garden; the foliage will stay neat and green year-round and the flowers are attractive for an extended period.

You can also use sea-pink in rock gardens or beside stony paths, where it flourishes due to the excellent drainage. Sea-pink is a natural for seaside gardens; it tolerates salty soil and sea spray. It combines well with blue false indigo (*Baptisia australis*) and white peonies.

GROWING AND PROPAGATION Plant in full sun and well-drained sandy or loamy soil. Avoid fertilizing, which can cause the foliage to flop open in the center. Once growing vigorously, this plant seldom needs watering. Remove faded flowerstalks regularly to extend bloom. Divide plants in the fall to renew them or to increase your supply of sea-pink.

Plant Profile

HARDINESS
Zones 3-8

SEASON OF BLOOM
Late spring and summer

LIGHT REQUIREMENTS
☼ ◑ ●
✓

MOISTURE REQUIREMENTS
◊ ◒ ◆
✓ ✓

HEIGHT
8-15 inches

SPREAD
8-10 inches

Artemisia spp.
ARTEMISIA

Highlight your perennial garden all season long with the aromatic silver foliage of artemisia.

The graceful silver foliage of 'Powis Castle' artemisia can become leggy. To prevent this, cut back old or winter-damaged plants in late spring.

Silvermound artemisia (A. *schmidtiana*; Zones 3 to 7) grows into a low mound to 2 feet tall.

GARDEN USES Use low-growing artemisias such as silvermound artemisia to edge a flower or herb garden, or in front of shrubs. They look great with lavender and pink yarrows. Use taller artemisias such as 'Powis Castle' to provide contrast with the green foliage of black-eyed Susans (*Rudbeckia* spp.) or bronze foliage of 'Palace Purple' heuchera (*Heuchera* 'Palace Purple'). 'Silver King' and 'Silver Queen' make bold groundcovers for sunny areas.

Plant Profile

HARDINESS
Zones 3-9

SEASON OF BLOOM
Summer and fall

LIGHT REQUIREMENTS
☼ ◑ ●
✓

MOISTURE REQUIREMENTS
◊ ◑ ●
✓ ✓

HEIGHT
1-4 feet

SPREAD
18 inches - 4 feet

APPEARANCE Artemisia's most striking feature is its silver foliage, which adds sparkle to any garden. One of the best is 'Powis Castle' (Zones 5 to 8), which can grow 3 feet tall and 4 feet wide, bearing finely cut silvery white foliage.

'Silver King' and 'Silver Queen' are both splendid cultivars of A. *ludoviciana* that reach 2 to 4 feet tall and spread rampantly.

GROWING AND PROPAGATION Plant in full sun and average, well-drained soil. Avoid fertilizing. Divide artemisias as needed to control size and keep growth compact and upright. Propagate shrubby 'Powis Castle' by taking stem cuttings rather than dividing. Cut back as needed to keep the plants neat.

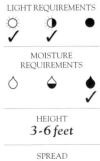
Aruncus dioicus
GOAT'S BEARD

*Give a lightly shaded garden an elegant centerpiece
with the feathery, creamy white spires of this
stately perennial.*

Goat's beard plants come in male and female forms. Male plants like these produce showier flower plumes, but flowers on female plants turn into lovely ornamental seedheads.

APPEARANCE Feathery white flower plumes rise over fernlike foliage. Each leaf has many broad, oval leaflets; leaves extend up to 3 feet long. Goat's beard may grow only 3 feet tall, but can reach as tall as 6 feet. One reliably compact cultivar is 'Kneiffii', which grows to 3 feet tall.

GARDEN USES Goat's beard provides impressive foliage and big, bold flowers to brighten up lightly shaded areas. Plant it at the rear of a large perennial garden or use it in large sweeps around trees or at the edge of a woodland. Goat's beard also grows well on the north side of a house; a dark-colored house shows off the white flowers. Good companion plants include European wild ginger (*Asarum europaeum*), lungworts (*Pulmonaria* spp.), and bleeding hearts (*Dicentra* spp.).

GROWING AND PROPAGATION Grow in light shade, or sun in cool climates, and moist, rich soil. Goat's beard seldom needs division, but you can divide it if you want more plants.

Plant Profile

HARDINESS
Zones 3-7

SEASON OF BLOOM
Late spring and early summer

LIGHT REQUIREMENTS

MOISTURE REQUIREMENTS

HEIGHT
3-6 feet

SPREAD
3-5 feet

Asarum spp.
WILD GINGER

The appealing heart-shaped leaves of this woodsy groundcover look cool and lush at the feet of shrubs or the edge of a shady garden.

Use European wild ginger as a low groundcover in wild, shaded areas for four-season interest.

Plant Profile

HARDINESS
Zones 3-8

SEASON OF BLOOM
Spring

LIGHT REQUIREMENTS
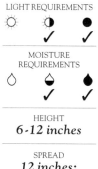

MOISTURE REQUIREMENTS

HEIGHT
6-12 inches

SPREAD
12 inches; clumps up to several feet

APPEARANCE Wild gingers have handsome leaves that can spread in colonies to form impressive sweeps of greenery. The ground-level flowers are small, rounded, and red-purple.

European wild ginger (A. *europaeum*; Zones 4 to 8) has shiny, evergreen, kidney-shaped leaves that form low masses to 8 inches tall.

Canada wild ginger (A. *canadense*) can reach 12 inches tall and bears lightly hairy, gray-tinted, heart-shaped leaves up to 6 inches long; the foliage lasts through the growing season and dies back in the fall.

Mottled wild ginger (A. *shuttleworthii*, also sold as *Hexastylis shuttleworthii*) has heart-shaped evergreen leaves with white mottling. 'Callaway' is a vigorous cultivar that spreads to form an attractive groundcover to 8 inches tall.

GARDEN USES Wild gingers are wonderful for providing green foliage or groundcover in shady sites. They make handsome additions to wildflower gardens and good companions for other shade-loving flowers such as wild blue phlox (*Phlox divaricata*) and Virginia bluebells (*Mertensia virginica*).

GROWING AND PROPAGATION Wild ginger needs shade and moist, rich, well-drained soil. Spread an inch or more of compost as a mulch around plants every year to maintain a high level of organic matter in the soil and irrigate as necessary during dry weather. To increase your supply of plants, divide when the foliage begins to die back in fall or as new growth begins in early spring. Handle the brittle roots carefully so you don't break them. In ideal locations, wild ginger may self-sow and spread moderately.

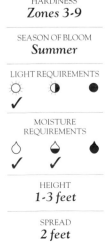

Asclepias tuberosa
BUTTERFLY WEED

*Bring monarchs and other butterflies to your garden
with the nectar-rich, incredible orange flowers of
summer-blooming butterfly weed.*

Butterfly weed has clusters of star-shaped orange flowers that open in early summer.

APPEARANCE Butterfly weed has flat-topped, rounded clusters of small orange flowers that butterflies adore. The flowers mature into slender upright pods with tapered ends. They open to release kid-pleasing seeds clad in downy parachutes. Butterfly weed grows from 1 to 3 feet tall and has long, narrow leaves. 'Gay Butterflies' is a mix of orange-, red-, and yellow-flowered plants that average 2 feet tall.

GARDEN USES Use butterfly weed in the middle or back of a flower border where its upright shape contrasts nicely with low or mound-shaped plants. It is right at home in a sunny meadow garden too. Surefire companions include coreopsis and black-eyed Susans (*Rudbeckia* spp.).

GROWING AND PROPAGATION Plant in full sun and average, well-drained soil. Remove the faded flowers in early summer to encourage rebloom in late summer. Butterfly weed may self-sow; removing the seedpods will keep it in check. If you don't mind a few volunteer self-sown plants, leave the interesting seedpods in place instead of snipping them off. Butterfly weed grows from a carrotlike taproot that doesn't transplant well. For best results, start with young plants and leave them undisturbed in the garden. If you want to increase your supply of plants, take tip cuttings in late spring or early summer or sow fresh seed outdoors in the late fall. If plants are troubled by aphids, spray them with insecticidal soap.

Plant Profile

HARDINESS
Zones 3-9

SEASON OF BLOOM
Summer

LIGHT REQUIREMENTS
○ ◑ ●
✓

MOISTURE REQUIREMENTS
◌ ◐ ●
✓ ✓

HEIGHT
1-3 feet

SPREAD
2 feet

Aster spp.

ASTER

These tough but beautiful daisylike flowers offer plenty of color and height choices to add long-lasting, often late-season bloom to a sunny bed or border.

The glowing flowers of 'Alma Potschke' New England aster can warm the grayest fall day.

Plant Profile

HARDINESS
Zones 3-8

SEASON OF BLOOM
Summer and fall

LIGHT REQUIREMENTS
☀ ◐ ●
✓

MOISTURE REQUIREMENTS
◊ ◖ ◆
✓ ✓

HEIGHT
1-6 feet

SPREAD
3-4 feet

APPEARANCE Some species of asters have daisylike flowerheads. Others are full and rounded like a chrysanthemum.

Long-blooming Frikart's aster (*A. x frikartii*; Zones 5 to 8) has lavender daisylike flowers from summer into fall on plants 2 to 3 feet tall. 'Monch' has blue flowers; 'Wonder of Staffa' has large blossoms.

New England asters (*A. novae-angliae*) have flowers of pink, white, lavender, and purple. They tend to be tall, averaging 3 to 6 feet. 'Alma Potschke', which has long-blooming pink flowers, grows 3 to 4 feet tall. One exception is the cultivar 'Purple Dome', which remains a compact 2 feet tall and has rich, deep purple flowers.

There are several compact cultivars of New York aster (*A. novi-belgii*), such as red 'Jenny', that grow to 1 foot tall.

GARDEN USES Use low fall-blooming asters in the front of a flower garden and tall fall asters in the back. They make ideal companions for artemisias and ornamental grasses. Frikart's aster is a great partner for orange coneflower (*Rudbeckia fulgida*) and 'Autumn Joy' sedum. You can also include asters in a meadow garden.

GROWING AND PROPAGATION These asters all require full sun and average to fertile soil. Frikart's aster is best in well-drained soil with modest moisture. New England and New York asters prefer evenly moist soil. Fertilize modestly or not at all. Use grow-through wire cages or rings to prevent tall asters from flopping. It also helps to pinch the new growth back a few inches in spring to encourage the plants to branch and stay compact.

New England and New York asters may need to be divided every 3 years to renew growth and control their spread. Frikart's aster seldom needs division. Some asters are prone to powdery mildew, but 'Purple Dome' is usually mildew-free. To discourage mildew, space plants so they do not touch.

Astilbe spp.
ASTILBE

Moisture-loving astilbes are a natural choice to plant beside a pond or water garden, where you can enjoy the reflections of their eye-catching flower clusters and rich foliage.

APPEARANCE Astilbes have erect or arching plumes of tiny flowers that brighten up any shady garden.

A. x *arendsii* grows from 2 to 4 feet tall, depending on the cultivar. Cultivars may bloom early, midseason, or late, and come in pink, white, red, and lilac.

Star astilbe (A. *simplicifolia*; Zones 5 to 8) reaches a petite 12 inches tall. 'Sprite' has delightful light pink flowers.

Chinese astilbe (A. *chinensis* var. *pumila*; Zones 3 to 8) is a low, spreading plant with pink flowers from 1 to 2 feet tall late in summer.

Thunberg's astilbe (A. *thunbergii*; Zones 4 to 8) can reach 2 to 3 feet tall and boasts handsome cascading flowers in mid- to late summer. 'Professor van der Weilen' is a white form.

For late-summer bloom, try fall astilbe (A. *taquetii*; Zones 4 to 8), which can reach 4 feet tall when in bloom.

GARDEN USES Use astilbes in a shady garden or on the north side of a house or wall. Let them sweep around stream or pond banks. Use compact astilbes in the front of a flowerbed and taller ones toward the back. They look great with lungworts (*Pulmonaria* spp.) and hostas. Astilbes also look lovely beneath trees or shrubs, but water regularly because the tree and shrub roots will compete for moisture.

'Fanal' is a compact, early-flowering cultivar of *Astilbe* x *arendsii* with deep crimson flowers.

GROWING AND PROPAGATION Plant in light shade and rich, moist soil (fall astilbe can tolerate occasional dry conditions). Water whenever the soil begins to get dry; brown leaf edges are a sign of underwatering. Mulch with an inch or more of compost and sidedress with an inch of aged manure in spring. Divide as needed to control size and multiply your astilbe collection. If the plant becomes hollow in the center, dig the center out, refill the space with rich soil, and allow the astilbe to fill in again.

Plant Profile

HARDINESS
Zones 3-9

SEASON OF BLOOM
Late spring and summer

LIGHT REQUIREMENTS
☼ ☽ ●
✓ ✓ ✓

MOISTURE REQUIREMENTS
◌ ◓ ◆
✓

HEIGHT
8 inches - 4 feet

SPREAD
2 feet

Athyrium spp.

LADY FERN, JAPANESE PAINTED FERN

Plant these gorgeous ferns along a path where their lacy fronds can be best admired.

Lady fern thrives in moist soils, forming dense mounds of delicate green fronds.

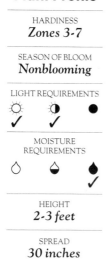

Plant Profile

HARDINESS
Zones 3-7

SEASON OF BLOOM
Nonblooming

LIGHT REQUIREMENTS
☀ ✓   ◐ ✓   ●

MOISTURE
REQUIREMENTS
◌   ◒   ◆ ✓

HEIGHT
2-3 feet

SPREAD
30 inches

APPEARANCE These ferns have leafy fronds that are twice-divided, creating a full and delicate effect. In ideal conditions, they will spread to form large colonies.

Lady fern (A. *filix-femina*) has broad, soft green fronds growing gracefully upright to as tall as 3 feet.

Japanese painted fern (A. *goeringianum* 'Pictum') has striking leaves tinged with purple and splashed with silver; the new growth is a handsome lavender shade and the silver variegation glows in a shady woodland garden. Its arching fronds spread to 2 feet tall and 30 inches wide.

GARDEN USES Lady ferns are as lovely in a shady foundation planting as in a woodland garden. Use them to offer interesting texture at the base of a tree trunk or include them among woodland wildflowers such as bloodroot (*Sanguinaria canadensis*), foamflowers (*Tiarella* spp.), and wild blue phlox (*Phlox divaricata*).

GROWING AND PROPAGATION Plant in rich, moist soil in light shade; in cool climates, lady fern can grow in sun. Irrigate and mulch with compost or shredded leaves to keep the soil constantly moist. Divide plants in early spring as new fronds are about to arise.

Baptisia australis
BLUE FALSE INDIGO

Add height and interesting texture to perennial beds with the cloverlike leaves and striking blue flowers of blue false indigo.

Blue false indigo flowers add valuable early-summer color to a bed or border, but the blue-green foliage is an asset too.

APPEARANCE Blue false indigo has spikes of bright blue flowers that rise from 2 to 4 feet tall. The blue-green leaves, which resemble clover, were once fermented to produce a blue dye. The dark seedpods remain interesting long after the flowers have faded.

GARDEN USES Use blue false indigo in the middle or rear of a flower garden. The cool blue flowers are a perfect complement to pink peonies, bleeding hearts (*Dicentra* spp.), and cranesbills (*Geranium* spp.). They contrast nicely with silver artemisia foliage or with golden and orange flowers, such as fernleaf yarrow (*Achillea millefolium*).

GROWING AND PROPAGATION Plant in sun or light shade and fertile, moist but well-drained soil. In shady sites, let the plant grow up through a supporting ring or grid. Deadhead to encourage long bloom or allow the seedpods to form for summer and fall interest. This is one perennial that stays put in the garden and won't require division. To increase your supply of plants, take cuttings from the tips of stems after flowering ends.

Plant Profile

HARDINESS
Zones 3-9

SEASON OF BLOOM
Late spring and early summer

LIGHT REQUIREMENTS
☼ ◑ ●
✓

MOISTURE REQUIREMENTS
◊ ◊ ◆
✓ ✓

HEIGHT
2-4 feet

SPREAD
3-4 feet

Brunnera macrophylla
SIBERIAN BUGLOSS

Enjoy the clear blue old-fashioned flowers of Siberian bugloss in early spring, then let the showy leaves fill in to command attention all season in a shady garden.

Siberian bugloss has pretty blue spring flowers and grows well in moist, shady spots.

Plant Profile

HARDINESS
Zones 3-8

SEASON OF BLOOM
Early spring

LIGHT REQUIREMENTS

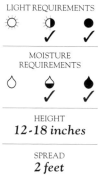

MOISTURE
REQUIREMENTS

HEIGHT
12-18 inches

SPREAD
2 feet

GARDEN USES Use Siberian bugloss in large clumps or as an edging near the front of a shady flower or shrub garden. It's an interesting companion to epimediums (*Epimedium* spp.) and Japanese painted fern (*Athyrium goeringianum* 'Pictum'). Siberian bugloss also looks beautiful in a woodland garden with bloodroot (*Sanguinaria canadensis*), wild blue phlox (*Phlox divaricata*), and ferns.

GROWING AND PROPAGATION

APPEARANCE Cheerful sprays of blue flowers arise in early spring along with many wildflowers. When they fade, heart-shaped leaves increase in size, reaching 12 to 18 inches tall. They remain handsome for the rest of the growing season. Variegated cultivars with white-marked leaves, such as 'Variegata' or 'Hadspen Cream', are especially attractive and brighten up any shady spot.

Plant in light shade and moist, rich but well-drained soil. In cool climates, Siberian bugloss can tolerate quite a bit of sun. In warm climates, give it full shade. Help the foliage reach full size by keeping the soil moist and adding compost and mulch. Irrigate during dry weather to prevent the foliage from dying back. For more plants, divide in late summer or early spring.

Calamagrostis x *acutiflora*
FEATHER REED GRASS

*Add flair to a perennial garden on a moist site
with the vertical line and showy flowers of
feather reed grass.*

APPEARANCE Feather reed grass forms a dense, grassy clump that reaches about 2 feet tall and may remain green year-round in mild climates. Feathery reddish flowerstalks grow to 5 feet tall, drying to a straw color for winter. 'Karl Foerster' has upright foliage and flowers that remain colorful all summer.

C. *arundinacea* 'Overdam', a similar species, has white-variegated leaves and golden flowers to 3 feet tall.

GARDEN USES 'Karl Foerster' feather reed grass is nice in the middle or rear of a flower garden where it forms a billowing backdrop for perennial flowers. Combine it with pink summer bloomers, such as phlox, Stokes' aster (*Stokesia laevis*), and pink balloon flower (*Platycodon grandiflorus*). You can also use this lovely grass as a low screen or herbaceous hedge. Or plant it with tall prairie perennials, such as black-eyed Susans (*Rudbeckia* spp.), in a meadow garden.

GROWING AND PROPAGATION Plant in moist but well-drained soil in full sun or light shade. Use a wide spacing to allow some elbowroom around the plants, which will improve air circulation and help prevent rust disease. If you want to cut back the flowerstalks, do so in early spring before new growth starts. Propagate by division in the spring or fall.

The upright stems of 'Karl Foerster' feather reed grass add striking vertical accents to a perennial border.

Plant Profile

HARDINESS
Zones 5-9

SEASON OF BLOOM
Early summer

LIGHT REQUIREMENTS
☼ ◑ ●
✓

MOISTURE REQUIREMENTS
◇ ◐ ◆
✓

HEIGHT
2-5 feet

SPREAD
2-3 feet

Cimicifuga racemosa
BLACK SNAKEROOT

Liven up lightly shaded areas near trees with the white-flowered candles of this attention-getting native wildflower.

Cimicifuga ramosa
'Atropurpurea', a relative of black snakeroot, has purplish leaves topped by tall spikes of creamy white flowers.

Plant Profile

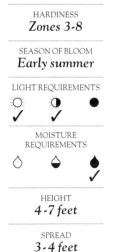

HARDINESS
Zones 3-8

SEASON OF BLOOM
Early summer

LIGHT REQUIREMENTS
✓ ✓

MOISTURE REQUIREMENTS
✓

HEIGHT
4-7 feet

SPREAD
3-4 feet

APPEARANCE Black snakeroot has long spires of small white flowers that tower 5 to 7 feet over the bushy, compound foliage. Bugbane (*C. japonica*), a related species, reaches 2 to 3 feet tall and produces white flowers in late summer or early fall.

Kamchatka bugbane (*C. simplex*) flowers in fall, reaching up to 6 feet high. 'White Pearl' is a compact version to 3 feet tall.

GARDEN USES The tall white flower spikes provide an impressive upright accent for lightly shaded gardens or woodland edges. Use black snakeroot for height around trees or in the rear of a large garden. It makes a good partner for astilbes, hostas, and ferns.

GROWING AND PROPAGATION Plant in sun or light shade and moist, rich, well-drained soil. Remove faded flowerstalks after bloom is finished. The plants mature into a single large clump that will continue to grow well without being divided. If you want to increase your supply of plants, you can divide in the fall; be sure that each division has at least one bud.

Convallaria majalis
LILY-OF-THE-VALLEY

*This old-fashioned charmer with fragrant flowers makes a
great groundcover for shady corners of the yard
where it's difficult to mow.*

Lily-of-the-valley bears charming bell-like flowers in spring. It spreads rapidly to form an attractive groundcover.

APPEARANCE Spikes of fragrant, white, bell-shaped flowers arise from paired, upright sword-shaped leaves that spread into large colonies. The flowers mature into red berries, which extend the season of interest. The plant, however, is poisonous and the berries can attract the attention of young children; clip the berries off if you think they'll be a temptation.

GARDEN USES Lily-of-the-valley flowers are renowned for their fabulous perfume, which is wonderful in the garden. Let the plants spread across the front of shade gardens or serve as a groundcover beneath trees or shrubs. Lily-of-the-valley looks good with spring-flowering bulbs, such as tulips, and with early-flowering perennials, such as lungworts (*Pulmonaria* spp.).

GROWING AND PROPAGATION Under ideal conditions of light shade and fertile, moist but well-drained soil, lily-of-the-valley will spread vigorously. It will also grow in full shade (especially in warm climates) and in sun in cool northern climates, and it will adapt to dry or average soils. If you interplant lily-of-the-valley with less aggressive plants, limit its spread with a root barrier, such as a plastic edging strip. Divide in spring or fall to keep in bounds and create new plants.

Plant Profile

HARDINESS
Zones 2-8

SEASON OF BLOOM
Spring

LIGHT REQUIREMENTS
✓ ✓ ✓

MOISTURE REQUIREMENTS
✓ ✓ ✓

HEIGHT
6-8 inches

SPREAD
Clumps spread to several feet

Coreopsis spp.

COREOPSIS, TICKSEED

Brighten a sunny garden with an armful of cheerful golden flowers from the versatile coreopsis clan.

'Golden Showers' threadleaf coreopsis has an airy beauty, with soft mounds of foliage covered in starry yellow flowers.

Plant Profile

HARDINESS
Zones 3-9

SEASON OF BLOOM
Late spring and summer

LIGHT REQUIREMENTS
☀ ◑ ●
✓

MOISTURE REQUIREMENTS
◊ ◊ ◊
✓ ✓

HEIGHT
1-3 feet

SPREAD
1-3 feet

APPEARANCE Coreopsis have bright yellow or golden flowers that bloom much of the summer.

Bigflower coreopsis (*C. grandiflora*; Zones 4 to 9), which has elongated, often lobed leaves, reaches to 2 feet tall and bears great masses of deep yellow flowers. Cultivars include 'Early Sunrise' and compact 'Goldfink', which only reaches 9 inches tall.

Lance-leaved coreopsis (*C. lanceolata*; Zones 3 to 8) is similar to bigflower coreopsis and is sometimes confused with it. One popular cultivar is 'Sunray'.

Threadleaf coreopsis (*C. verticillata*) has short, fine leaves and forms an airy mound up to 3 feet tall. 'Moonbeam' has pastel yellow flowers. 'Zagreb' has golden flowers and reaches only 18 inches tall.

Pink tickseed (*C. rosea*; Zones 4 to 8) is a standout with pink flowers to 2 feet tall and fine, needlelike foliage.

GARDEN USES Use coreopsis in any sunny situation that calls for a long-blooming perennial. They fit well into a foundation planting and are perfect for the front or middle of a flower garden. They're also ideal in a meadow garden. All coreopsis combine beautifully with violet sage (*Salvia x superba*) and blue balloon flower (*Platycodon grandiflorus*). In a garden of warm colors, plant coreopsis with crocosmias and butterfly weed (*Asclepias tuberosa*).

GROWING AND PROPAGATION Plant in full sun (pink tickseed also grows in light shade), in average, well-drained soil. Stems may flop if the soil is too rich. Allow room around lance-leaved coreopsis plants to discourage powdery mildew. Divide coreopsis in spring or fall if they are declining or to increase your supply of plants. Trim back faded flowers to encourage rebloom. Some coreopsis cultivars can flower until frost.

Corydalis lutea
YELLOW CORYDALIS

Try the fine-textured foliage of corydalis as a groundcover or filler in a shady garden and enjoy a bonus of yellow blooms.

Yellow corydalis blooms from spring until fall, making it an invaluable addition for shady gardens with rich soil.

APPEARANCE Yellow corydalis has small, tubular flowers and handsome blue-green compound leaves similar to columbines (*Aquilegia* spp.). It can bloom for months. The flowers are lemon yellow and abundant on the spreading plant, which can reach to 15 inches tall in bloom.

For a similar look with blue flowers, try *C. flexuosa* 'Blue Panda'. It reaches only 8 inches tall and produces sky blue flowers through the growing season.

GARDEN USES Use yellow corydalis for a bright touch in the foreground of any shady garden, foundation planting, or woodland scene. It looks great with bleeding hearts (*Dicentra* spp.), Siberian bugloss (*Brunnera macrophylla*), ferns, and hostas.

GROWING AND PROPAGATION Plant in rich, moist but well-drained soil in light or full shade. Yellow corydalis can self-sow heavily. Allow the extra seedlings to expand the planting, or transplant them to a new site. Remove faded flowers occasionally to encourage rebloom and limit self-seeding.

Plant Profile

HARDINESS
Zones 5-7

SEASON OF BLOOM
Late spring, summer, and fall

LIGHT REQUIREMENTS

MOISTURE REQUIREMENTS

HEIGHT
9-15 inches

SPREAD
18 inches

Crambe cordifolia
COLEWORT

Add flair to a sunny perennial border with colewort's enormous leaves and surprisingly delicate cloud of white flowers.

Colewort has massive branches of white flowers that erupt in summer and then disappear when the spent flower stems are cut back.

Plant Profile

HARDINESS
Zones 4-7

SEASON OF BLOOM
Early summer

LIGHT REQUIREMENTS
☀ ◑ ●
✓

MOISTURE REQUIREMENTS
◌ ◗ ●
✓

HEIGHT
3-7 feet

SPREAD
4 feet

APPEARANCE Colewort sports broad, toothed leaves to 2 feet wide that spread into a large rosette up to 4 feet across. Airy sprays of small white flowers, like baby's-breath, rise above the foliage, reaching 5 to 7 feet tall.

GARDEN USES Plant colewort in the rear or middle of a flower border for a magnificent flower display. The airy blossoms make a nice backdrop for upright flowers such as early phlox (*Phlox maculata*) and violet sage (*Salvia* x *superba*). Colewort retains its interesting bold leaves throughout the growing season.

GROWING AND PROPAGATION Plant in sun and rich, moist soil, allowing enough space for the plants to expand. Fertilize in spring and irrigate to keep the soil constantly moist. Stake the bloom stalks to keep upright and cut them back after the flowers fade. Control cabbage moth caterpillars by applying insecticidal soap.

Crocosmia spp.
CROCOSMIA

*Draw hummingbirds like a magnet with the
vivid orange, red, and yellow spikes
of crocosmia.*

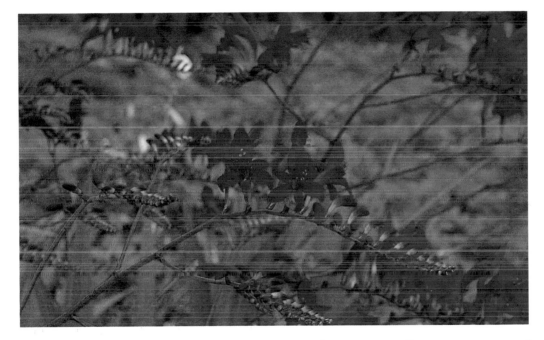

**Fiery red
'Lucifer'**
crocosmia
makes an eye-
catching
addition to beds
and borders.

APPEARANCE Crocosmias have upright fans of foliage similar to Siberian iris (*Iris sibirica*) and bold spikes of gold, red, and orange flowers.

Light orange 'Citronella' and yellow 'Solfatare' are cultivars of C. x *crocosmiiflora* (Zones 6 to 9), which grows up to 3 feet tall.

Some of the most magnificent crocosmias are hybrids such as C. 'Lucifer', which grows 3 to 3½ feet tall and has vivid red flowers.

GARDEN USES Use crocosmias for an upright accent among mounding and spreading perennials such as 'Moonbeam' coreopsis (*Coreopsis verticillata* 'Moonbeam'), daylilies, and Stokes' aster (*Stokesia laevis*). Crocosmias are a must in a hummingbird garden.

GROWING AND PROPAGATION
Crocosmias grow from corms, similar to crocuses. Plant in spring, providing full sun and moist, rich well-drained soil. The corms will multiply, producing tight, showy clumps of plants. In cold climates, dig up the corms and store them in a cool, dry basement during winter. Divide in the fall to renew the plants or to increase your supply. If spider mites become a problem, spray them with insecticidal soap.

Plant Profile

HARDINESS
Zones 5-9

SEASON OF BLOOM
Summer

LIGHT REQUIREMENTS
☼   ◑   ●
✓

MOISTURE
REQUIREMENTS
◊   ◓   ◆
✓

HEIGHT
2-3½ feet

SPREAD
1-2 feet

$C\ r\ o\ c\ u\ s$ spp.
CROCUS

This group of bulbs includes both early spring bloomers and fall-blooming types to accent perennial gardens or to naturalize in the lawn.

Dutch crocuses planted in random clusters in your lawn will make a cheerful spring display.

Plant Profile

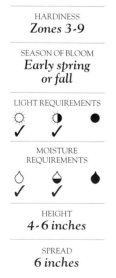

HARDINESS
Zones 3-9

SEASON OF BLOOM
Early spring or fall

LIGHT REQUIREMENTS

MOISTURE REQUIREMENTS

HEIGHT
4-6 inches

SPREAD
6 inches

APPEARANCE Petite bowl-shaped flowers open on sunny early spring days. The foliage is narrow and straplike with a white stripe down the center of each leaf. The earliest-blooming species have smaller flowers. They include golden crocus (*C. chrysanthus*; Zones 4 to 9), which grows to 6 inches tall, and its cultivars, such as yellow 'Goldilocks', blue 'Blue Bird', and purple 'Skyline'.

Dutch crocus (*C. vernus*) and Dutch hybrid crocuses (*C. vernus* subsp. *vernus* hybrids) flower slightly later and often have larger blooms. They include cultivars such as lavender 'Enchantress', 'Violet

Vanguard', 'Yellow Mammoth', and 'Queen of the Blues'. More unusual fall-blooming species include the saffron crocus (*C. sativus*; Zones 5 to 9) and the showy crocus (*C. speciosus*; Zones 5 to 9).

GARDEN USES Plant crocuses at the perimeter of your lawn, beneath shade trees, or around spring-flowering shrubs. Put crocuses near a walk, doorway, or window where you can enjoy their flowers first thing in spring. If you plant crocuses at a distance from your house, use brightly colored, large-flowered types in big groups. Plant them in large sweeps between clumps of perennials such as daylilies and hosta. Use them in combination with larger bulbs such as daffodils by planting the crocuses in a shallow layer over the more deeply planted bulbs.

GROWING AND PROPAGATION Plant crocuses in sun or light shade in average, well-drained soil. Crocuses grow from bulblike corms, which you plant in fall. Let the crocus foliage die back before removing it; delay mowing if the crocuses are planted in the lawn. To keep chipmunks or other rodents from eating the corms, enclose the corms in a cage of fine wire mesh. Fertilize in spring with ½ inch of aged manure or compost. Divide if overcrowded or to expand your collection.

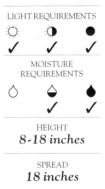

Dicentra spp.
BLEEDING HEART

*Remember yesteryear with the pretty foliage and dainty,
arching stems of pink or white bleeding hearts in your
favorite shady spot.*

APPEARANCE Heart- or tear-shaped flowers are trademarks of this perennial. They emerge on arching stems over handsome compound foliage.

One of the best is wild bleeding heart (*D. eximia*), which reaches from 10 to 18 inches tall. It produces modest but abundant pink tear-shaped flowers much of the spring and summer. 'Alba' has white flowers. The hybrid cultivar 'Luxuriant' grows 12 to 18 inches tall and has red-pink flowers that are at their best in cool weather.

Dutchman's breeches (*D. cucullaria*; Zones 3 to 8) is a wildflower that can reach 12 inches tall. It is peppered with small dangling white or yellowish white pouchlike flowers. Squirrel corn (*D. canadensis*; Zones 4 to 7) is similar with greenish white flowers. Both of these plants go dormant in early summer.

GARDEN USES Use bleeding hearts in the front or middle of any shade garden. They are naturals for wildflower gardens, where some species provide extended color after spring bloomers fade. Combine bleeding hearts with wild gingers (*Asarum* spp.), yellow corydalis (*Corydalis lutea*), 'Sulphureum' Persian epimedium (*Epimedium* × *versicolor* 'Sulphureum'), and ferns.

The delicate flower sprays and soft foliage of wild bleeding heart mix beautifully with fern fronds.

GROWING AND PROPAGATION Plant in light to full shade; in warm climates, morning sun is fine. Plant in moist, rich soil and mulch with compost. Irrigate during dry weather. Mark the location of squirrel corn and Dutchman's breeches so you don't damage underground plant parts after the tops die back. To increase your supply of plants, divide clumps or take root cuttings in the fall.

Plant Profile

HARDINESS
Zones 3-9

SEASON OF BLOOM
Spring and summer

LIGHT REQUIREMENTS
☼ ◑ ●
✓ ✓ ✓

MOISTURE REQUIREMENTS
○ ◒ ●
  ✓ ✓

HEIGHT
8-18 inches

SPREAD
18 inches

Echinacea purpurea
PURPLE CONEFLOWER

Fill your summer gardens with this pink-purple daisy and you'll get a bonus of nectar-seeking butterflies and seed-eating goldfinches.

The pink petals of 'Bright Star' purple coneflower seem to almost glow next to its rich orange-brown cones.

Plant Profile

HARDINESS
Zones 3-8

SEASON OF BLOOM
Summer

LIGHT REQUIREMENTS
☀ ◑ ●
✓

MOISTURE REQUIREMENTS
◊ ◖ ◆
✓ ✓

HEIGHT
2-4 feet

SPREAD
1-2 feet

APPEARANCE This native American prairie plant has flashy red-purple petals surrounding an orange-red central cone. The flowering stems can reach 3 to 4 feet tall but seldom need staking for support. The pointed oval leaves are large and somewhat hairy. Once the flowers fade, the cones remain, becoming darker with maturity and attracting foraging birds when the seeds ripen. 'White Lustre' has white flowers. 'Bright Star' has rose-pink flowers. 'Magnus' has a dark central disk.

GARDEN USES Use purple coneflowers in the middle to rear of any sunny flower border. For a lovely trio, plant purple coneflowers with orange coneflowers (*Rudbeckia fulgida*) and coreopsis or with balloon flowers (*Platycodon grandiflorus*) and asters. You can also use purple coneflowers in meadow gardens with ornamental grasses and other prairie plants.

GROWING AND PROPAGATION Plant in full sun and average, well-drained soil. Irrigate during dry weather. Remove faded flowers to prolong bloom. The cones will add winter interest if you let them stand, and you'll get a bonus of self-sown seedlings in spring and summer. If you need more plants, simply transplant the seedlings. Plants often decline after division.

Epimedium spp.
EPIMEDIUM

*Try epimediums for a lovely groundcover that
produces a flurry of small columbine-like flowers in
a shade garden.*

APPEARANCE The main attraction of epimediums is their handsome heart-shaped foliage, which often is tinted with red. The small flowers, shaped like jesters' caps, are often hidden among the leaves; some gardeners clip the leaves short so the flowers will be easier to see.

Long-spurred epimedium (*E. grandiflorum*) reaches 8 to 15 inches tall with pink, purple, or white flowers. Red epimedium (*E. x rubrum*) grows to 12 inches tall with bronze-painted spring foliage and red flowers.

Young's barrenwort (*E. x youngianum*) reaches 8 inches tall. 'Roseum' has pink flowers. Extra-early-flowering 'Niveum' has white flowers.

'Sulphureum' Persian epimedium (*E. x versicolor* 'Sulphureum') has soft yellow flowers on plants that grow to 12 inches tall.

GARDEN USES Epimedium's pretty, deciduous to evergreen foliage makes an attractive groundcover or edging for any shade garden. It grows especially well around trees and shrubs, situations where it's often difficult to establish groundcovers. Combine epimedium with spring-flowering bulbs such as daffodils and squills (*Scilla* spp.) for a riot of spring color and appealing greenery through the rest of the season.

'Sulphureum' Persian epimedium has bronze-tinged leaves that look beautiful in the garden and also in cut flower arrangements.

GROWING AND PROPAGATION Plant in light to full shade and moist, fertile soil. Many epimediums can grow in less than ideal soil, even in dry sites riddled with woody plant roots. They spread slowly to colonize wide areas. To speed up their spread, divide plants in late summer and transplant. Cut back any tattered foliage in spring before growth resumes.

Plant Profile

HARDINESS
Zones 4-8

SEASON OF BLOOM
Spring

LIGHT REQUIREMENTS

MOISTURE REQUIREMENTS

HEIGHT
6-15 inches

SPREAD
8-15 inches

Eranthis hyemalis
WINTER ACONITE

Tuck winter aconite tubers under trees or at the front of perennial gardens where it's easy to spot their low yellow flowers in early spring.

Winter aconites are such early bloomers that late-season storms may leave their yellow blossoms surrounded by snow.

Plant Profile

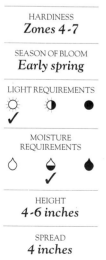

HARDINESS
Zones 4-7

SEASON OF BLOOM
Early spring

LIGHT REQUIREMENTS

MOISTURE
REQUIREMENTS

HEIGHT
4-6 inches

SPREAD
4 inches

APPEARANCE This petite, early spring bloomer has clusters of yellow buttercup-like flowers 4 to 6 inches tall above a frill of divided foliage. *E. cilicica* is an old-fashioned yellow-flowering species only 2 inches tall.

GARDEN USES Put large sweeps of winter aconites in the front of flower or shrub beds or swirl them around clumps of perennials such as Lenten rose (*Helleborus orientalis*), hosta, or Siberian iris (*Iris sibirica*). They look great with other early-spring bulbs such as daffodils or purple and blue crocuses.

GROWING AND PROPAGATION Buy fresh tubers and soak briefly before planting. Plant winter aconite tubers in fall, in light shade or sun, in rich, moist but well-drained soil. Keep sunny locations moist by mulching and irrigating during dry weather. They may flower poorly the first year after planting, but each year their display will improve. Once growing well, winter aconites may reseed and expand generously. After 3 years of growth, winter aconites are ready for dividing. To rejuvenate old clumps or increase your supply, divide clumps in fall by breaking the tubers into several pieces.

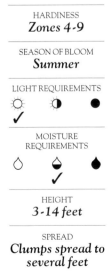
Eupatorium fistulosum
JOE-PYE WEED

The shrublike proportions and huge mauve flower puffs of Joe-Pye weed make a magnificent backdrop to a sunny perennial garden.

Spotted Joe-Pye weed sports umbrella-like flower clusters in late summer.

APPEARANCE Lofty heads of red-purple flowers top stems of long leaves, which may appear in pairs along the stems or encircle the stems in groups. Plants can grow 5 to 14 feet tall.

Related species include spotted Joe-Pye weed (*E. maculatum*; Zones 2 to 8), which reaches 4 to 6 feet tall and has slightly smaller flowerheads, and sweet Joe-Pye weed (*E. purpureum*; Zones 3 to 8), which ranges from 3 to 6 feet tall with modest-sized clusters of pastel pink or purple flowers.

GARDEN USES Use Joe-Pye weed in the rear of a flower border or in a prairie garden. It also thrives in moist areas, such as along creeks or ponds, where it makes an ideal companion to Siberian iris (*Iris sibirica*) and daylilies.

GROWING AND PROPAGATION Plant in full sun or light shade and rich moist soil. Joe-Pye weed seldom needs fertilizing. To reduce height, pinch back new growth in spring to encourage branching. Irrigate during dry weather to help plants grow to their maximum height. Divide in spring as needed to control spread or to increase your supply of plants. Deadhead to prevent self-sowing.

Plant Profile

HARDINESS
Zones 4-9

SEASON OF BLOOM
Summer

LIGHT REQUIREMENTS
☼ ◑ ●
✓

MOISTURE REQUIREMENTS
◊ ◊ ◆
✓

HEIGHT
3-14 feet

SPREAD
Clumps spread to several feet

Geranium spp.
CRANESBILL, HARDY GERANIUM

Plant a variety of cranesbills for weeks of cheerful blooms and intriguing foliage that offers great red or orange fall color.

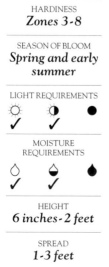

'Wargrave Pink' Endress cranesbill makes a long-blooming groundcover that's perfect along a sunny pathway.

Plant Profile

HARDINESS
Zones 3-8

SEASON OF BLOOM
Spring and early summer

LIGHT REQUIREMENTS
☀ ◐ ●
✓ ✓

MOISTURE REQUIREMENTS
◊ ◒ ◆
✓ ✓

HEIGHT
6 inches - 2 feet

SPREAD
1-3 feet

APPEARANCE Cranesbills are low-growing perennials that have saucer-shaped flowers and rounded leaves that may be lobed or finely cut. The common name cranesbill comes from the seedpod, which resembles the beak of a crane.

Endress cranesbill (G. *endressii*; Zones 4 to 8) has starlike leaves and bears pink flowers. It can reach 18 inches tall. 'A. T. Johnson' has light salmon-pink flowers; 'Wargrave Pink' bears rich pink flowers.

Blood-red cranesbill (G. *sanguineum*) grows to 12 inches tall with bold pink flowers and deeply cut leaves.

Cultivars include 6-inch-tall 'Shepherd's Warning' and white 'Album'.

G. *renardii* (Zones 4 to 8) has gray leaves and purple-veined white flowers to 8 inches tall.

Wild cranesbill (G. *maculatum*; Zones 4 to 8) has light pink, purple, or white flowers, and rises to 2 feet tall.

Bigroot cranesbill (G. *macrorrhizum*) forms a groundcover with pink flowers to 18 inches tall.

'Biokovo' (Zones 4 to 8) is a hybrid cultivar that has pastel pink flowers and evergreen foliage. 'Johnson's Blue' (Zones 4 to 8) has beautiful blue flowers on plants to 18 inches tall.

GARDEN USES Use cranesbills in the front or middle of flower borders, around shrubs or small ornamental trees, or beside a walk or retaining wall. Wild cranesbill looks great in a wildflower garden.

GROWING AND PROPAGATION
Cranesbills grow in sun to partial shade in almost any well-drained soil. Gray-leaf types need fast-draining soils. Remove faded flowers on 'Johnson's Blue' and Endress cranesbill cultivars to extend the flowering season. Divide in spring or late summer to control the spread of quick growers such as bigroot cranesbill or to increase your collection.

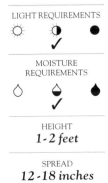
Helleborus spp.
HELLEBORE

*Get the jump on the garden season with hellebores,
which have beautiful foliage and roselike flowers that bloom
in winter and early spring.*

APPEARANCE These cheerful and showy bowl-shaped flowers appear very early in the growing season. The deeply lobed leaves are dark green and may be evergreen in warm climates.

Corsican hellebore (*H. argutifolius*; Zones 6 to 8) can grow over 2 feet tall with large clusters of spring green flowers.

Christmas rose (*H. niger*; Zones 3 to 8) reaches 18 inches tall. In late winter (or early spring in cold climates) it produces clear white flowers that fade to pink.

Lenten rose (*H. orientalis*; Zones 4 to 9) grows 12 to 18 inches tall with white, green, pink, or purple flowers or combinations of these colors.

GARDEN USES Plant hellebores close to your house, patio, or walk so you'll get maximum early-season enjoyment from the flowers. They also add a nice touch between shrubs in a foundation planting. Use the plants singly or in sweeps. Combine them with other early bloomers such as early-season daffodils, crocuses, squills (*Scilla* spp.), and winter aconites (*Eranthis* spp.).

GROWING AND PROPAGATION Plant in rich, moist but well-drained soil in light or medium shade. Cultivate the soil deeply before planting because hellebores produce a long taproot. Mulch to keep the soil moist, discourage weeds, and prevent the flowers

from being stained by mud if they bow down near the soil. Irrigate during dry weather for at least the first 2 years after planting. Corsican hellebore may need staking to hold the flowers upright. Remove tattered evergreen leaves at the end of winter. Avoid dividing or transplanting hellebores. If you want to increase your supply of plants, you can transplant any self-sown seedlings that may appear.

Lenten rose flowers in shades ranging from white to purple. If you want specific colors, buy plants in bloom.

Plant Profile

HARDINESS
Zones 3-9

SEASON OF BLOOM
Winter and spring

LIGHT REQUIREMENTS
☼ ◑ ●
✓

MOISTURE REQUIREMENTS
◇ ◉ ⬤
✓

HEIGHT
1-2 feet

SPREAD
12-18 inches

Hemerocallis spp.
DAYLILY

Cover a slope with the lively green leaves and trumpetlike flowers of daylilies, or use them as an accent in foundation plantings and island beds.

Fast-spreading tawny daylilies are a good choice for a tough site where touchier perennials won't grow well.

APPEARANCE Open trumpet-shaped flowers appear in spring and summer over clumps of arching, straplike leaves. Plants can grow from 1 to 5 feet tall. You can grow old-fashioned species such as orange-flowered tawny daylily (*H. fulva*) or modern hybrids, which come in an incredible variety of colors, shapes, and sizes.

One of the earliest daylilies to flower is the lemon daylily (*H. lilioasphodelus;* Zones 3 to 9). It has perfumed yellow flowers on 3-feet-tall plants.

Hybrids flower in shades of yellow, orange, pink, red, green, ivory, and purple. 'Mary Anne' is pink; 'Palest Yellow' is an off-white. 'Stella de Oro' is a compact 2-foot-tall daylily with yellow-orange flowers that rebloom through the summer.

'Happy Returns', another rebloomer, has lemon yellow flowers. Miniature daylilies such as 'Shortee' grow only a foot tall.

GARDEN USES Use daylilies in any flower garden or mixed garden of flowers, shrubs, and trees. Combine them with purple coneflowers (*Echinacea purpurea*), butterfly weed (*Asclepias tuberosa*), and gayfeathers (*Liatris* spp.). Try planting spring-flowering bulbs such as daffodils or tulips around the perimeter of a daylily clump. Use daylilies as groundcovers on banks or other open areas.

GROWING AND PROPAGATION

Daylilies will thrive in a wide variety of soils and exposures, from sand to clay and sun to light shade. But an ideal site has sun and moist, rich, well-drained soil. In light shade, daylilies may flower less and be likely to flop. Fertilize in spring or mulch with compost. In summer, remove faded flowers and old flowerstalks to keep the plants tidy. If aphids infest new growth or buds, spray with insecticidal soap. Divide fast-growing daylilies such as 'Stella de Oro' every 3 years. Other types can go for years without division. To divide a mature clump, hose off the exposed roots and saw apart the root mass with a sturdy, sharp knife. Replant young, healthy sections and compost the older parts.

Plant Profile

HARDINESS
Zones 2-9

SEASON OF BLOOM
Spring and summer

LIGHT REQUIREMENTS

MOISTURE REQUIREMENTS

HEIGHT
1-5 feet

SPREAD
2-3 feet

Heuchera spp.
CORAL BELLS, HEUCHERA

Enjoy the delicate beauty of red and pink coral bells rising above neat scalloped leaves, and watch for the hummingbirds that adore the flowers.

APPEARANCE Coral bells have dainty spikes of small bell-shaped flowers that bloom above a tidy rosette of deciduous to evergreen leaves.

Coral bells (H. *sanguinea*; Zones 4 to 9) produce white, pink, or red flowers that reach to 18 inches tall over handsome scalloped leaves.

Hybrid coral bells (H. x *brizoides*; Zones 3 to 8) are more heat tolerant and provide many bright-flowered cultivars including pink 'Chatterbox'.

American alumroot (H. *americana*; Zones 3 to 8) produces small green flowers to 3 feet tall.

'Palace Purple' heuchera (Zones 4 to 8) has purple or bronze leaves and small white flowers.

GARDEN USES Use coral bells as an edging for any flower or shrub bed. Combine with other spring bloomers with attractive leaves, such as cranesbills (*Geranium* spp.) and Siberian bugloss (*Brunnera macrophylla*). Plant 'Palace Purple' with contrast color perennials such as yellow coreopsis or silver artemisia.

GROWING AND PROPAGATION Plant in sun to partial shade and moist, rich, well-drained soil. Remove faded flower stems after blooming to keep the plants neat and encourage rebloom. If strawberry root weevils chew notches out of leaves and tunnel through crowns, apply beneficial nematodes. The color and quality of 'Palace Purple' can vary; look for vegetatively propagated forms with good purple foliage, and plant in light shade in warm climates to maintain the color. Divide every 3 years to keep plants growing well.

Coral bells have bright pink flowers in late spring. They make a charming edging for perennial beds and borders.

Plant Profile

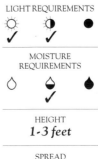

HARDINESS
Zones 3-9

SEASON OF BLOOM
Spring and summer

LIGHT REQUIREMENTS

MOISTURE REQUIREMENTS

HEIGHT
1-3 feet

SPREAD
12-18 inches

Hosta spp.

HOSTA

*Depend on these unbeatable foliage
plants for cool elegance in your
shade gardens.*

Add excitement to shade gardens with variegated hostas like 'Albo-marginata' Fortune's hosta.

Plant Profile

HARDINESS
Zones 3-8

SEASON OF BLOOM
Summer

LIGHT REQUIREMENTS

MOISTURE REQUIREMENTS

HEIGHT
6 inches - 3 feet

SPREAD
6 inches - 5 feet

APPEARANCE Hostas are renowned for their foliage – stylish leaves that range from small to gigantic, smooth-textured to puckered, in green, gold, blue, or white. There are hundreds of different types.

'So Sweet' has white-edged leaves to 18 inches tall with fragrant white flowers. 'Ginko Craig' has white-edged, lance-shaped leaves and purple flowers.

Fortune's hosta (*H. fortunei*) grows to 2 feet tall with long, heart-shaped leaves and soft lilac flowers. 'Albo-marginata' has white-rimmed leaves.

'Elegans' Siebold's hosta (*H. sieboldiana* 'Elegans') can reach 3 feet tall with blue-green leaves and light lavender flowers in late summer.

Seersucker hosta (*H. sieboldii*) grows to 30 inches tall with broad crinkled leaves.

Blue hosta (*H. ventricosa*) rises to 3 feet tall with large leaves and blue-purple flowers.

GARDEN USES Use low-growing hostas as an edging or in clusters near the front of a flower or shrub garden. Larger hostas make bold accents rising above ground-covers such as bigroot cranesbill (*Geranium macrorrhizum*), epimediums (*Epimedium* spp.), and foamflowers (*Tiarella* spp.). Use large- to medium-sized hostas in the middle or back of a shady flower garden, with companions such as lady fern (*Athyrium filix-femina*) and wild bleeding heart (*Dicentra eximia*).

GROWING AND PROPAGATION Plant in light to full shade in moist, rich, well-drained soil. Once established, many hostas can withstand dry conditions. Fertilize in spring, and mulch with compost. If slugs are a problem, remove the mulch and trap slugs with beer traps (margarine tubs of beer set with the rim at soil level). Or surround your hostas with copper strips, which slugs will not cross. Hostas seldom need dividing, but you can multiply your collection by slicing off a rooted wedge from a mature plant in late summer.

Iris sibirica
SIBERIAN IRIS

The commanding swordlike leaves and rich flower color of Siberian iris make a great accent in a perennial garden or a lush natural planting near a water garden.

APPEARANCE Flowers shaped like a fleur-de-lis are composed of three petals pointing down and three petals pointing up. They bloom abundantly over clumps of tall, grassy foliage. Plants can reach from 1 to 3 feet tall. Siberian iris blooms in purple, lavender, blue, yellow, white, and red, plus combinations of these colors. Light blue 'Baby Sister', one of the shortest, reaches 12 inches. 'Little White' grows to 15 inches tall. 'Caesar's Brother' reaches 24 inches with dark purple flowers. 'Tycoon' has deep blue-purple flowers to 36 inches tall. Some new cultivars, such as white 'Marshmallow Frosting' and red 'Reddy Maid', have thicker petals and stalks.

GARDEN USES Siberian irises are great in any flower garden, whether they're standing alone, in clumps, or in masses. Plant dwarf types in the foreground and taller cultivars in the background. Their upright form contrasts well with mounded plants such as coreopsis and cranesbills (*Geranium* spp.). They also grow beautifully on stream or pond banks combined with Joe-Pye weeds (*Eupatorium* spp.) and daylilies.

GROWING AND PROPAGATION Plant in full sun in moist, rich soil. They will also tolerate light shade. Well-drained soil is best, but Siberian irises can tolerate

occasionally wet soils. Irrigate to keep the soil evenly moist for the first season after planting, and subsequently during dry spells. In early summer, remove and destroy any leaves streaked with brown tunnels, signs of iris borer attack. Remove all leaves in fall to eliminate iris borer eggs. Siberian irises seldom need division, but if you want to expand your planting, you can divide them in spring or late summer.

Siberian irises like 'Caesar's Brother' tolerate a wide range of conditions and thrive in almost any perennial border.

Plant Profile

HARDINESS
Zones 2-9

SEASON OF BLOOM
Early summer

LIGHT REQUIREMENTS
✓

MOISTURE REQUIREMENTS
✓

HEIGHT
1-3 feet

SPREAD
1-2 feet

Lavandula angustifolia
LAVENDER

The wonderful fragrance of lavender's silvery foliage and blue-purple flowers is an extra treat in a sunny garden.

Lavender flowers attract butterflies and bees, and add beauty and fragrance to both cut and dried flower arrangements.

GARDEN USES Lavender is a natural choice for cottage or herb gardens where its fragrance is as important as its bright silvery gray foliage. Set it beside paths so it will release its perfume when you brush by. Plant a row of lavender plants together to form a low hedge. Combine with pink-flowered yarrow, blue Russian sage (*Perovskia atriplicifolia*), and pink peonies, which provide contrast with their dark green foliage.

GROWING AND PROPAGATION
Lavender needs full sun. It does best in fast-draining sandy soil. If you don't have sandy loam soil, plant lavender in a raised bed for good drainage, and amend the soil with coarse sand. You can also mulch with coarse sand to keep the base of the plant extra dry. In cold climates, cover plants with evergreen boughs after the soil freezes to limit winter damage. After new leaves emerge in late spring, trim off the previous season's dead foliage. Prune to shape, as needed. Remove faded flower spikes to keep plants neat. Increase your supply of lavender by dividing in early spring, or by taking cuttings from the tips of new stems in the fall and rooting them in pots.

Plant Profile

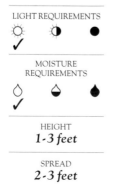

HARDINESS
Zones 5-9

SEASON OF BLOOM
Summer

LIGHT REQUIREMENTS
☀ ◐ ●
✓

MOISTURE REQUIREMENTS
◇ ◖ ◆
✓

HEIGHT
1-3 feet

SPREAD
2-3 feet

APPEARANCE Bushy plants 2 to 3 feet tall bear aromatic silver, needlelike leaves. Fragrant spikes of small flowers in blue, purple, or lavender arise in midsummer; cultivars with white or pink flowers are less common, but available. Cultivars include 'Hidcote', which grows to 15 inches tall and has purple flowers; 'Munstead', to 18 inches with lavender flowers; and 'Jean Davis', to 18 inches with light pink flowers.

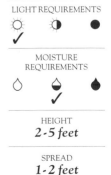

Liatris spp.
GAYFEATHER, BLAZING STAR

Vivid spires of intense purple-pink flowers make gayfeathers a natural choice for accenting a sunny bed or border.

APPEARANCE Gayfeathers have fluffy spikes of bright purple-pink flowers atop stems covered with grasslike leaves. White-flowered cultivars are available for most species.

Spike gayfeather (*L. spicata*) reaches 2 to 3 feet tall with midsummer flower spikes about 2 feet long. 'Kobold' is a compact cultivar that grows to 30 inches tall.

Tall gayfeather (*L. scariosa*; Zones 4 to 9) reaches 3 feet tall with pale purple flowers in late summer.

Kansas gayfeather (*L. pycnostachya*) grows 3 to 5 feet tall and blooms in summer.

GARDEN USES The upright form of gayfeathers stands out in the middle or rear of any flower garden. They contrast well with mounded or low-growing plants such as daylilies, cranesbills (*Geranium* spp.), and pincushion flower (*Scabiosa caucasica*). Try gayfeathers in meadow gardens with black-eyed Susans (*Rudbeckia* spp.) and asters. The blooms also attract butterflies.

GROWING AND PROPAGATION Grow gayfeathers in sun and average, well-drained soil. In moist and fertile soils, stake the plants to prevent them from flopping over when in bloom. Water during drought, using trickle irrigation to

discourage rust disease. Gayfeathers seldom need division but if you need to expand your planting, you can divide in spring or late summer.

'Kobold' spike gayfeather produces glowing mauve-pink blooms for several weeks beginning in midsummer.

Plant Profile

HARDINESS
Zones 3-9

SEASON OF BLOOM
Summer

LIGHT REQUIREMENTS
✓

MOISTURE
REQUIREMENTS
✓

HEIGHT
2-5 feet

SPREAD
1-2 feet

Mentha spp.
MINT

Mints have a delightfully refreshing scent, but they spread wildly, so plant them in a spot where they can extend their creeping stems at will.

Mint has attractive flowers for cutting as well as aromatic foliage to spice up concoctions from your kitchen.

Plant Profile

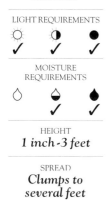

HARDINESS
Zones 4-9

SEASON OF BLOOM
Summer

LIGHT REQUIREMENTS

MOISTURE REQUIREMENTS

HEIGHT
1 inch-3 feet

SPREAD
Clumps to several feet

APPEARANCE There are dozens of aromatic mints; all have opposite leaves and square stems. They bear spikes of tiny, two-lipped flowers.

Variegated pineapple mint (M. *suaveolens* 'Variegata') smells like apple and has handsome variegated leaves that reach to 16 inches tall.

Peppermint (M. x *piperita*), 18 to 36 inches tall, has smooth flavorful leaves and purple stems.

Spearmint (M. *spicata*) has toothed, lightly hairy leaves on stems that grow up to 36 inches tall.

Corsican mint (M. *requienii*; Zones 6 to 9) is a ground-hugging type only an inch tall.

GARDEN USES Use mints in shady herb gardens or as a quick-spreading groundcover for a moist, shady location. Try creeping Corsican mint between stones in a walk. White-variegated pineapple mint makes an appealing addition to the middle of a perennial border. It looks great with white Siberian iris (*Iris sibirica*) or early phlox (*Phlox maculata*) in a sunny garden, or with white-variegated hosta in a shade garden.

GROWING AND PROPAGATION Mints grow best in rich, moist soil and light to medium shade, but many will also thrive in full sun and less than ideal conditions. They are notorious spreaders that reroot from any broken pieces of stem or root left in the soil. To prevent rampant growth in a perennial garden, plant mints in bottomless nursery pots. Leave the pot rim an inch or more above the soil surface, and check often to make sure the spreading stems don't escape over the rim of the pot (cut back any that do). Divide confined plants every 2 years to keep them vigorous.

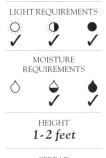

Mertensia virginica
VIRGINIA BLUEBELL

*Add the finishing touch to a shady garden
with the gorgeous blue blossoms of this
beloved wildflower.*

Virginia bluebells have dainty pink flower buds that change to blue as they open in spring.

APPEARANCE Clusters of nodding pink flower buds that open to blue bell-shaped flowers form at the top of the stems. The leaves are soft and oval. Plants reach to 2 feet when in flower, then quickly die back to the ground until next year.

GARDEN USES Grow Virginia bluebells with other woodland wildflowers, such as bloodroot (*Sanguinaria canadensis*) and Solomon's seals (*Polygonatum* spp.), on wooded banks, near streams, and in moist meadows. Plant them between perennials such as ferns, cranesbills (*Geranium* spp.), or hostas. When planted in a favorable site, Virginia bluebells can spread into a thick spring carpet of exceptional beauty.

GROWING AND PROPAGATION Virginia bluebells thrive in light shade but can also grow in sun if the soil is kept moist. Provide fertile soil rich in organic matter and good drainage. Be sure to mark the location of the plants so you won't damage them by digging into them when they are dormant. The plants will self-sow as long as the soil isn't mulched heavily. To increase your supply of plants, divide large clumps after they flower.

Plant Profile

HARDINESS
Zones 3-9

SEASON OF BLOOM
Spring

LIGHT REQUIREMENTS
✓ ✓ ✓

MOISTURE REQUIREMENTS
✓ ✓

HEIGHT
1-2 feet

SPREAD
1-2 feet

Miscanthus sinensis
JAPANESE SILVER GRASS

*Plant long-lived Japanese silver grass to add structure
and a sense of motion to a mixed border or
pondside garden.*

'Morning Light' is an excellent cultivar of Japanese silver grass that creates a fountain of white-edged foliage.

Plant Profile

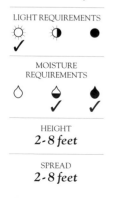

HARDINESS
Zones 5-8

SEASON OF BLOOM
Summer and fall

LIGHT REQUIREMENTS
☼ ◐ ●
✓

MOISTURE REQUIREMENTS
◊ ◖ ◆
  ✓ ✓

HEIGHT
2-8 feet

SPREAD
2-8 feet

APPEARANCE This ornamental grass has clumps of upright leaves rising 4 to 8 feet tall. Feathery pink or red flower plumes open in fall and ripen to soft tan, remaining attractive all winter. There are many fine cultivars to choose from. 'Purpurascens', to 4 feet tall, has foliage that turns red in summer or fall and pink flowers in August. Compact 'Yaku Jima' has silvery leaves and red flowers reaching to 4 feet tall. 'Adagio' has silver-gray leaves and grows only 2 feet tall. 'Morning Light' grows to 5 feet tall with fine-textured, white-edged leaves.

Porcupine grass (*M. sinensis* var. *strictus*) has yellow-banded leaf blades and a bold, upright shape.

Zebra grass (*M. sinensis* 'Zebrinus') has similar yellow-banded blades but grows in an open shape to 6 to 7 feet tall.

GARDEN USES Japanese silver grass provides beautiful movement in a perennial garden when the breeze rustles its long leaves and flower plumes. Most dry well to a buff color and remain attractive deep into winter. Use them in the back of a flower or shrub garden, or make them a backdrop for perennials such as Siberian iris (*Iris sibirica*), Russian sage (*Perovskia atriplicifolia*), and 'Autumn Joy' sedum. They make instant summer privacy screens and special accents beside a stream or pond.

GROWING AND PROPAGATION Plant in sun and average, well-drained soil. Cut back old foliage to 4 to 6 inches tall in spring before growth resumes. Fertilize lightly in spring. To keep foliage in a tight clump, divide every 3 years in the spring.

Muscari spp.
GRAPE HYACINTH

Scatter grape hyacinths through bulb plantings and wildflower gardens for early spring color of a delightful deep blue.

Armenian grape hyacinth sends up leaves in the fall, and then blooms in early spring, producing grapelike blue flowers.

APPEARANCE Spikes of small bell-shaped flowers, 6 to 8 inches tall, arise early in spring and continue to flower for weeks. Most cultivars have deep blue flowers, but there also are white and pink forms.

Armenian grape hyacinth (*M. armeniacum*) is the standard blue grape hyacinth. 'Cantab' has lighter blue flowers. *M. botryoides* has light blue flowers. 'Album' has bright white flowers.

GARDEN USES Plant large sweeps of grape hyacinths around clumps of perennials and shrubs. They look especially pretty with other spring bloomers such as lungworts (*Pulmonaria* spp.) and Siberian bugloss (*Brunnera macrophylla*). To create a mixed bulb planting, plant grape hyacinth bulbs in a shallow layer over larger bulbs such as daffodils or tulips.

GROWING AND PROPAGATION Plant grape hyacinth bulbs in the fall, in sun to light shade in average, well-drained soil. Mark the location of the bulbs so you don't disturb them when they're lying dormant in summer and fall. To expand your planting, divide bulbs in early summer after the tops die back. You can divide grape hyacinths as often as every 4 years.

Plant Profile

HARDINESS
Zones 4-8

SEASON OF BLOOM
Spring

LIGHT REQUIREMENTS

MOISTURE REQUIREMENTS

HEIGHT
6-8 inches

SPREAD
6 inches

Narcissus spp.
DAFFODIL

Plant generous handfuls of daffodil bulbs in your perennial garden for a spring show of cheerful blossoms that return year after year.

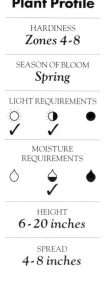

Miniature daffodils like 'Jack Snipe' are a good choice for mixed borders because the foliage dies back quickly after their delicate flowers fade.

Plant Profile

HARDINESS
Zones 4-8

SEASON OF BLOOM
Spring

LIGHT REQUIREMENTS
☀ ✓ ◐ ✓ ●

MOISTURE REQUIREMENTS
◇ ◑ ✓ ◆

HEIGHT
6-20 inches

SPREAD
4-8 inches

Unusual hybrid double-flowered forms include fragrant gold-and-white 'Cheerfulness'. Species daffodils are smaller.

Triandrus daffodils such as white 'Thalia' and tazetta daffodils like miniature 'Minnow' produce clusters of flowers on each flowering stem. Another popular miniature is golden 'Tête-à-Tête', which reaches 6 inches tall.

GARDEN USES Use daffodils throughout flower and shrub gardens, planting sweeps of bulbs around clumps of daylilies or hostas. They combine beautifully with blue-flowered Siberian bugloss (*Brunnera macrophylla*). Plant in large clumps of seven or more bulbs of a single cultivar for impressive color. Plant trumpet daffodils in open woodlands or the edges of your lawn. For extended bloom season, use early, midseason, and late-blooming cultivars.

GROWING AND PROPAGATION Plant bulbs in fall in sun or light shade and average, well-drained soil. Apply an inch of compost after bloom to improve flowering on older plantings. Allow the foliage to yellow before removing it. To renew a sparse-flowered planting, divide the bulbs as foliage dies back in summer. Mark location of dormant bulbs to avoid damaging them in summer or fall.

APPEARANCE Familiar trumpet flowers appear on upright stems in spring, in sunny yellow, white, orange, pink, or two-tones. Straplike leaves grow in upright clumps. While there are more than 50 naturally occurring species of daffodils, most of the popular cultivars are hybrids.

Traditional hybrid trumpet daffodils rise to 20 inches tall. Some excellent cultivars include 'Salome', with a salmon trumpet ringed by white petals; all-white 'Mount Hood'; or 'King Alfred' type daffodils, which have golden flowers.

Osmunda cinnamomea
CINNAMON FERN

*Add interesting color accents and fine texture to moist,
shaded gardens with the waist-high fronds of these
beautiful ferns.*

APPEARANCE Cinnamon fern can grow from 2 to 5 feet tall in a spreading vase shape. Showy stalks of cinnamon-colored spore clusters come up first in the spring, followed by the yellow-green or dark green fronds.

Interrupted fern (*O. claytoniana*; Zones 2 to 8) is a related fern that has a similar look but stays about 3 feet tall. The spore-bearing segments on each frond fall off early in the growing season, leaving a gap along the stalk.

Royal fern (*O. regalis*; Zones 2 to 10), which grows 3 to 6 feet tall, bears reddish-tinted young fronds that mature to green. Spore clusters form at the tips of the fronds instead of on separate stalks.

GARDEN USES Use these ferns in moist woodlands, boggy locations, or streamsides. They also are wonderful for shady foundation plantings beside perennials such as bleeding hearts (*Dicentra* spp.) and corydalis (*Corydalis* spp.).

Ferns like royal fern offer garden interest from the moment new fronds unfurl in early spring until they begin to die back in the fall.

GROWING AND PROPAGATION Plant in partial or full shade and moist, rich, acidic soil. They will tolerate some sun and average soil. Irrigate in dry weather to keep cinnamon ferns and royal ferns uniformly moist. To increase your supply of plants, lift an established fern, and use a sharp knife to cut it into several sections.

Plant Profile

HARDINESS
Zones 2-10

SEASON OF BLOOM
None

LIGHT REQUIREMENTS

MOISTURE
REQUIREMENTS

HEIGHT
2-5 feet

SPREAD
1 foot

Paeonia spp.
PEONY

These old-fashioned favorites add lush, romantic blooms to a sunny garden in early summer, and their shrubby foliage makes a great backdrop for later-blooming perennials.

Peonies produce impressive shrublike mounds of sculptured foliage that are a garden asset even after the sumptuous blooms fade.

Plant Profile

HARDINESS
Zones 2-8

SEASON OF BLOOM
Spring and early summer

LIGHT REQUIREMENTS
☼ ◑ ●
✓

MOISTURE REQUIREMENTS
◊ ◖ ◆
✓

HEIGHT
18 inches - 3 feet

SPREAD
3-4 feet

APPEARANCE Peony flowers may be elegant singles, full doubles, or interesting intermediate forms. The large blooms top a vigorous clump of stems covered in handsome divided leaves. New leaves emerge as showy red shoots in spring. The flowers put on a great display for a week or two, and the foliage stays attractive all season, turning bronze in fall.

Many popular peonies are hybrids of common peony (*P. officinalis*; Zones 3 to 8), which reaches 2 feet and blooms in late spring, and common garden or Chinese peony (*P. lactiflora*), up to 3 feet tall and blooming later. Both produce white, pink, or red flowers which often are fragrant.

Cultivars of the species have a wide range of flowering times, providing an extended peony season. Some classic cultivars of Chinese peony include 'Sarah Bernhardt', a midseason double pink, and 'Nippon Beauty', a modified single late red. 'Rubra Plena' is an early double red cultivar of common peony.

GARDEN USES Peonies are a great choice for the middle to rear of any flower garden. Let them stand alone or in groups with cranesbills (*Geranium* spp.), Siberian iris (*Iris sibirica*), and early phlox (*Phlox maculata*). Draw attention to the red spring shoots by planting Grecian windflower (*Anemone blanda*) or pasque flower (*Anemone pulsatilla*) around them.

GROWING AND PROPAGATION Plant in sun, in fertile, rich, moist but well-drained soil. Peonies can tolerate light shade, especially in warm climates. Fertilize with a balanced or high potassium organic fertilizer each spring, and irrigate during spring and late summer. Support plants with a grow-through ring. During wet weather the flower buds may blacken and die from botrytis disease. To prevent spread, remove the diseased buds immediately and destroy the foliage in fall. Ants may crawl on the buds but cause no harm. Peonies seldom need division, but if you want more plants, you can lift clumps in late summer and divide by cutting them into sections using a sharp knife.

Perovskia atriplicifolia
RUSSIAN SAGE

For an airy touch in a sunny perennial border, try the silvery foliage and delicate blue flower spikes of Russian sage.

Russian sage thrives on hot, dry sites and its silvery gray stems remain attractive long after the flowers fade.

APPEARANCE This bushy perennial grows 3 to 5 feet tall and produces long, slim sprays of small blue flowers at the top of the stems. The stems are covered with small, toothed, silvery leaves that have a mild sage fragrance. 'Blue Spire' has blue-purple flowers. 'Longin' grows into a more narrow, upright shape. 'Blue Mist' is an early bloomer with light blue flowers.

GARDEN USES Russian sage provides a satisfying summer show when it blooms at the rear of a large flower garden. Set it behind gold or pink yarrows and pink or purple asters. You can also plant large masses of Russian sage to create an informal hedge or screen.

GROWING AND PROPAGATION Grow Russian sage in sun and average, well-drained soil. It dies back to the ground in cold climates but may not in warm climates. If necessary, cut the plant back to 1 foot tall in spring before growth resumes. In shadier sites, stake the plant to keep it upright. Once established, Russian sage tolerates heat and drought. If you need more plants, take cuttings in early summer.

Plant Profile

HARDINESS
Zones 4-9

SEASON OF BLOOM
Summer

LIGHT REQUIREMENTS
☀ ◐ ● ✓

MOISTURE REQUIREMENTS
◇ ◖ ◆ ✓

HEIGHT
3-5 feet

SPREAD
3-5 feet

Phlox spp.
PHLOX

There's a phlox for every site in your yard — moss phlox to frost a slope with spring color, garden phlox to anchor a border, and wild blue phlox for shady gardens.

Wild blue phlox may die down in midsummer but will often regrow in the fall.

APPEARANCE All phlox species have tubular five-petaled flowers that flare out at the end to form a round face.

Spring-blooming phlox include creeping phlox (*P. stolonifera*; Zones 2 to 8), which grows to 8 inches tall and has purple, lavender, white, or pink flowers; wild blue phlox (*P. divaricata*; Zones 3 to 9), which fans up to 15 inches tall when its blue, white, or lavender flower sprays bloom; and moss phlox (*P. subulata*), which forms dense mats to 8 inches tall topped by pink, red, blue, or white flowers.

Early phlox (*P. maculata*; Zones 3 to 9) and garden phlox (*P. paniculata*; Zones 4 to 8) bloom in summer. Early phlox has narrow foliage and clusters of pink or white flowers to 3 feet tall. One great cultivar is pink-flowered 'Alpha'.

Garden phlox reaches to 4 feet tall and flowers in white, pink, purple, salmon, and combinations of these colors. Many cultivars are prone to powdery mildew. 'David' is a fragrant white-bloomer with mildew resistance.

GARDEN USES Use spring-flowering phlox as groundcovers or edgings for shrub or flower beds. Creeping phlox and wild blue phlox thrive in shade with other wildflowers such as Virginia bluebells (*Mertensia virginica*) and Solomon's seals (*Polygonatum* spp.). Moss phlox is ideal for a sunny bank or groundcover. Summer-flowering phlox are perfect for the middle to rear of a flower garden. Combine with low-growing cranesbills (*Geranium* spp.) and fall-blooming asters for a long-lasting color sequence.

GROWING AND PROPAGATION Grow wild blue phlox and creeping phlox in shade and moist, rich soil. Irrigate if needed during drought. Divide after flowering. Wild blue phlox may fall dormant in midsummer and regrow in fall.

Grow moss phlox in full sun and average, well-drained soil. Plant early and garden phlox in moist, fertile, well-drained soil in full sun. Divide these summer-blooming phlox every 4 years to renew their growth.

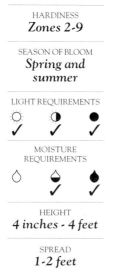

Plant Profile

HARDINESS
Zones 2-9

SEASON OF BLOOM
Spring and summer

LIGHT REQUIREMENTS
☼ ◑ ●
✓ ✓ ✓

MOISTURE REQUIREMENTS
◌ ◖ ◆
✓ ✓

HEIGHT
4 inches - 4 feet

SPREAD
1-2 feet

Platycodon grandiflorus
BALLOON FLOWER

This enchanting perennial has beautiful blue-purple or pink star-shaped flowers that bloom all summer in a sunny garden, plus lovely yellow foliage in fall.

APPEARANCE Balloon flower has remarkable inflated flower buds that look like miniature hot air balloons. They open to five-lobed, saucer-shaped flowers of rich blue or pink (the variety *albus* has white flowers). The flowers cluster at the end of stems 1 to 3 feet tall. The foliage is triangular and finely toothed. 'Fuji Blue' grows to 3 feet tall. For a fuller flower, try 'Double Blue', which reaches to 2 feet tall. The compact variety *mariesii* stays 18 inches tall. 'Shell Pink' has pink flowers on 2-foot-tall stems.

GARDEN USES Balloon flowers are beautiful in the middle or rear of any flower garden. The unusual flower buds are a delight for both children and adults. Combine balloon flowers with garden phlox, Japanese anemones (*Anemone* x *hybrida*), and cranesbills (*Geranium* spp.). They also look lovely against a backdrop of Japanese silver grass (*Miscanthus sinensis*) or with contrasting yellow yarrows.

GROWING AND PROPAGATION Plant in full sun and average, well-drained soil. Plants can become floppy if they receive too much shade and too much fertilizer.

Mark the site of your balloon flowers in fall, because they are late to emerge in spring and easy to damage by careless digging. Remove faded flowers to extend blooming season. Plants seldom need division, but if you want to make divisions to increase your supply of plants, you can lift clumps in spring or early fall. If you do, dig deeply to avoid damaging the thick roots.

If you want a balloon flower for the front of a perennial border, choose the compact variety *mariesii*.

Plant Profile

HARDINESS
Zones 3-8

SEASON OF BLOOM
Summer

LIGHT REQUIREMENTS
☼ ◐ ●
✓

MOISTURE REQUIREMENTS
◇ ◑ ◆
✓

HEIGHT
1-3 feet

SPREAD
1-2 feet

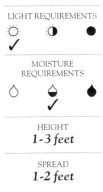

Polygonatum spp.
SOLOMON'S SEAL

Add a grace note to a shady garden with the tall arching stems and dangling bell-like flowers of Solomon's seals.

White leaf outlines add an artistic touch to the gently curving stems of variegated Solomon's seal.

Plant Profile

HARDINESS
Zones 3-9

SEASON OF BLOOM
Spring

LIGHT REQUIREMENTS

MOISTURE
REQUIREMENTS

HEIGHT
1-7 feet

SPREAD
2-4 feet

APPEARANCE Solomon's seal has upright stems that arch at the top in a graceful curve. Attractive oval leaves cover the stems.

Solomon's seal (*P. biflorum*) grows up to 3 feet tall and bears white, bell-shaped flowers that dangle from the underside of the arching stem. Great Solomon's seal (*P. biflorum* var. *commutatum*; Zones 3 to 7) is similar but grows 3 to 7 feet tall.

Variegated Solomon's seal (*P. odoratum* 'Variegatum') has eye-catching white-edged leaves, fragrant flowers, and stems to 30 inches tall.

GARDEN USES Let Solomon's seal provide an upright accent in your shade or wildflower garden. The foliage lasts through the summer and the flowers mature into handsome dark blue berries, providing interest after other wildflowers have gone dormant. For a pleasant combination of shapes, plant colonies of Solomon's seal with creeping wildflowers like creeping phlox (*Phlox stolonifera*) and mound-forming wildflowers like bloodroot (*Sanguinaria canadensis*).

GROWING AND PROPAGATION
Solomon's seal grows well in shade and moist, fertile soil. Irrigate during dry weather so the soil doesn't dry out. Plants can expand to form thriving colonies. Divide in spring or fall to restrict their size or expand your planting.

Pulmonaria spp.
LUNGWORT,
BETHLEHEM SAGE

Brighten the front of a shady garden with lungwort's striking silver-spotted foliage and soft blue spring flowers.

The narrow leaves of long-leaved lungwort (*Pulmonaria longifolia*) offer an interesting backdrop for its vivid spring flowers.

APPEARANCE Lungworts produce small, bell-shaped blue or pink flowers in spring. They continue to please garden visitors through the rest of the growing season with long oval- or lance-shaped foliage. The foliage of some species also has attractive silver markings.

Bethlehem sage (*P. saccharata*), to 18 inches tall, has pink buds and blue flowers. Cultivars with exceptional silver-marked leaves include 'Mrs. Moon' and 'Sissinghurst White', which has white flowers. Their foliage can last into winter in mild climates.

The hybrid cultivar 'Roy Davidson' has long narrow leaves mottled with silver and grows to 10 inches tall. The flowers open pink and turn to blue.

GARDEN USES Let lungworts carpet garden areas, spreading around the base of shrubs and trees or stretching across the front of flower gardens. They work well in a shady foundation planting, where you can enjoy the silver-marked foliage from your windows. Good companions include daffodils, tall astilbes, blue-leaved hostas, and Japanese painted fern (*Athyrium goeringianum* 'Pictum').

GROWING AND PROPAGATION Plant in shade, in moist, rich soil. Irrigate during dry weather to prevent plants from going dormant prematurely. Leaves may mildew or turn brown around the edges if water is scarce. Divide as needed to renew growth or expand your planting.

Plant Profile

HARDINESS
Zones 3-8

SEASON OF BLOOM
Spring

LIGHT REQUIREMENTS
☼   ◑ ✓   ● ✓

MOISTURE REQUIREMENTS
◌   ◑ ✓   ● ✓

HEIGHT
9-18 inches

SPREAD
2 feet

Rudbeckia spp.
BLACK-EYED SUSAN, RUDBECKIA

Black-eyed Susans have vibrant yellow flowers that carry a wave of color through the summer in a sunny garden.

Black-eyed Susans offer a long display of striking yellow flowers when planted in a warm, sunny spot with average soil.

Plant Profile

HARDINESS
Zones 3-9

SEASON OF BLOOM
Summer and fall

LIGHT REQUIREMENTS

MOISTURE REQUIREMENTS

HEIGHT
18 inches - 7 feet

SPREAD
2-3 feet

APPEARANCE Black-eyed Susan flowers have showy golden petals surrounding a dark center cone. Hairy oval- to lance-shaped leaves cover the upright stems.

Orange coneflower (*R. fulgida*) can grow to 3 feet tall with classic black-eyed Susan flowers. They bloom for about four weeks in mid- to late summer. The variety *sullivantii* produces larger flowers. 'Goldsturm' is a compact 2 feet tall with large flowers. If you want uniform plants, avoid 'Goldsturm Strain', which is grown from seed, and buy only plants of the named cultivar.

Shining coneflower (*R. nitida*; Zones 4 to 9) grows to 4 feet tall with leaves up to 1 foot long. The flowers have yellow petals and a green cone. 'Herbstsonne' can reach 7 feet tall and blooms in mid- to late summer.

GARDEN USES Black-eyed Susans work well in the middle to rear of any sunny flower garden and look wonderful with violet sage (*Salvia* x *superba*). You can mix black-eyed Susans with butterfly weed (*Asclepias tuberosa*), purple coneflower (*Echinacea purpurea*), and gayfeathers (*Liatris* spp.) in a meadow garden. Put groups of three or five black-eyed Susans between shrubs to brighten up a sunny foundation planting. The long-lasting seedheads attract birds and provide winter interest.

GROWING AND PROPAGATION Plant in full sun and average, well-drained soil. In rich soil, plants may become floppy and require staking. Remove faded flowers often to encourage extended bloom. But leave late-season flowers in place so their dark cones will add to your garden's winter display. Black-eyed Susans may self-sow; remove faded flowers if you can't find space for more seedlings. Plants spread moderately. Divide in spring to increase your plant supply or to control growth.

Salvia spp.
SALVIA, SAGE

*Include salvias in sunny borders for bold color,
aromatic foliage, and irresistible
hummingbird appeal.*

APPEARANCE Salvias are shrubby or mounded plants that have square stems, oval or lancelike leaves, and small tubular flowers that cluster at the stem tips.

Violet sage (*S.* x *superba*; Zones 4 to 7) grows to 3½ feet tall with leathery, triangular leaves and upright spikes of blue-violet flowers in summer. 'East Friesland', a compact favorite, grows to 18 inches tall.

Garden sage (*S. officinalis*) is a culinary herb with lance-shaped silver leaves and blue flowers. It can grow to 2 feet tall. 'Compacta' stays 8 inches tall; 'Berggarten' has round leaves; 'Purpurascens' has purplish leaves. 'Tricolor' blends pink, white, and green in its leaves. 'Icterina' has gold variegated foliage and is less hardy than the species.

You'll also find many lovely hybrid salvia cultivars. 'May Night' (also sold as 'Mainacht') has dark purple flowers to 14 inches tall. 'Rose Queen' has pink flowers to 24 inches tall.

GARDEN USES Garden sages are at home in any herb garden. You can also use them in flower gardens to add aroma and foliage color. Try purple-leaved 'Purpurascens' with yellow daylilies or coreopsis. Violet sage is a great choice for the middle of a flower border. It blends well with creeping plants such as bugleweed (*Ajuga* spp.) and

cranesbills (*Geranium* spp.) or mound-shaped plants such as 'Moonbeam' coreopsis and 'Autumn Joy' sedum.

GROWING AND PROPAGATION Plant sages in sun and well-drained soil. Garden sages do best in fast-drying, sandy soil of low fertility, especially during winter. Violet sages grow well in average soils. Remove faded flower spikes promptly on violet sage and it will rebloom. Divide plants in spring or fall to control their spread. To increase your supply of plants, take cuttings in early summer.

'May Night' salvia produces intense blue-purple flower spikes in summer. Deadhead fading flowers promptly to encourage continued bloom.

Plant Profile

HARDINESS
Zones 3-9

SEASON OF BLOOM
Summer and fall

LIGHT REQUIREMENTS
☀ ◐ ●
✓

MOISTURE REQUIREMENTS
◇ ◐ ◆
✓

HEIGHT
8 inches - 3½ feet

SPREAD
3 feet

Sanguinaria canadensis
BLOODROOT

Scatter bloodroot in shady woodland gardens or formal shade borders for white starry flowers in early spring.

Bloodroot has pristine white flowers that appear for a few days in early spring and attractive foliage that lasts into fall.

Plant Profile

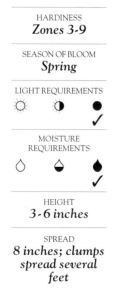

HARDINESS
Zones 3-9

SEASON OF BLOOM
Spring

LIGHT REQUIREMENTS

MOISTURE
REQUIREMENTS

HEIGHT
3-6 inches

SPREAD
8 inches; clumps spread several feet

APPEARANCE In sunny spring weather, white, bowl-shaped flowers emerge from inside the fold of a large, lobed, blue-green leaf. When the weather turns dark, cold, or wet, the leaf encloses the flowers again. This native wildflower grows to 6 inches tall and can spread to form large colonies. The foliage can last into summer, providing interesting greenery in a shady garden. Double-flowered 'Multiplex' has flowers that look like water lilies.

GARDEN USES Use clusters or sweeps of bloodroot in shady wildflower gardens or around spring-flowering shrubs or trees.

Ideal companions include Virginia bluebells (*Mertensia virginica*), wild cranesbill (*Geranium maculatum*), and Solomon's seals (*Polygonatum* spp.).

GROWING AND PROPAGATION Plant in a shady site with moist, rich, but well-drained soil. If you plant bloodroot under trees, avoid sites that are heavily riddled with roots, because the soil there can become dry and infertile. Irrigate during dry weather to prevent the foliage from dying back prematurely. Divide to increase your supply of plants when the foliage begins to die back in late summer.

Scabiosa caucasica
PINCUSHION FLOWER

*Plant a cluster of these lacy-flowered perennials
in a sunny garden and enjoy the pastel blossoms and the
butterflies they attract.*

Pincushion flowers look equally lovely in the garden and in cut flower arrangements.

APPEARANCE Flat, lacy flowerheads in blue, pink, or white appear in late summer over basal clusters of fuzzy, lance-shaped leaves. Plants can reach to 2 feet tall. 'Butterfly Blue' has lavender-blue flowers to 15 inches tall that appear most of the growing season. 'Pink Mist' is similar with purple-pink flowers. 'Alba' is a white-flowered form that grows to 2 feet tall.

GARDEN USES Use groups of three, five, or more pincushion flowers in the front or middle of a flower garden. Plant a large mixed cluster of 'Pink Mist' and 'Butterfly Blue' for an impressive display. Pincushion flowers also complement lavender or artemisias well. Or for contrast, try 'Butterfly Blue' with low-growing yellow daylilies.

GROWING AND PROPAGATION Grow pincushion flowers in sun and average, well-drained soil. In warm climates, choose a site that has afternoon shade. Remove faded flowers to encourage extended bloom. Divide in spring only if needed to renew growth. To increase your supply of plants, take stem cuttings in spring.

Plant Profile

HARDINESS
Zones 3-7

SEASON OF BLOOM
Spring, summer, and fall

LIGHT REQUIREMENTS
☼ ◐ ●
✓

MOISTURE REQUIREMENTS
◊ ◊ ◆
✓ ✓

HEIGHT
15 inches-2 feet

SPREAD
12-18 inches

Scilla spp.
SQUILL

Tuck dozens of these early-blooming bulbs under shrubs and trees where their starlike blue, pink, or white flowers will lift your spirits in spring.

Siberian squills carpet the ground with intense blue blossoms in spring. Use them in beds, borders, and container plantings.

Plant Profile

HARDINESS
Zones 3-8

SEASON OF BLOOM
Spring

LIGHT REQUIREMENTS
☼ ◐ ●
✓ ✓

MOISTURE REQUIREMENTS
◌ ◑ ●
✓

HEIGHT
6 inches

SPREAD
2-3 inches

APPEARANCE Siberian squills (*S. siberica*) bear nodding, blue, star-shaped flowers on stems to 6 inches tall. Each bulb also produces three or four strap-shaped leaves, which turn yellow and die by early summer. 'Spring Beauty' is a classic blue-flowered cultivar. 'Alba' has white flowers.

Spanish bluebells (once considered a species of *Scilla*, but now classified as *Hyacinthoides hispanicus*; Zones 4 to 8) look similar to Siberian squill, but each bulb sends up a sprawling clump of basal leaves and several flowerstalks up to 18 inches tall. The fragrant flowers may be blue, pink, white, or violet.

GARDEN USES Use squills to paint sweeps of spring color across the front of garden beds. Combine them with other early spring bloomers such as winter aconites (*Eranthis hyemalis*), crocuses, and Lenten rose (*Helleborus orientalis*). They also can thrive and spread in woodland gardens.

GROWING AND PROPAGATION Grow squills in sun to light shade and average, well-drained soil. In ideal conditions, squills will self-sow and expand in drifts. You can also enlarge a planting by dividing and replanting the bulbs every 2 years as the foliage dies back in summer.

Sedum spp.
SEDUM, STONECROP

Creeping sedums trailing over a rock wall soften the wall's sharp edges, while tall sedums lend four-season interest in perennial beds and borders.

APPEARANCE All sedums have fleshy leaves and clusters of small, star-shaped flowers. Creeping types grow to 6 inches tall, while upright sedums may reach 2 feet tall.

Three excellent creeping sedums are white stonecrop (*S. album*), Kamschatka sedum (*S. kamtschaticum*; Zones 3 to 8), and two-row sedum (*S. spurium*; Zones 3 to 8). White stonecrop bears evergreen leaves and white flowers.

Kamschatka sedum has yellow flowers and slim, scalloped leaves that change to red in fall. The cultivar 'Variegatum' has white-edged leaves.

Two-row sedum produces a carpet of round leaves, topped by pink flowers. Leaves of 'Tricolor' are colored green, pink, and white. 'Dragon's Blood' has bronze foliage and red flowers.

Showy stonecrop (*S. spectabile*) rises up to 2 feet tall in an open vase shape. It has large heads of pink or red flowers. 'Stardust' has white flowers.

The hybrid cultivar 'Autumn Joy' has fleshy round, toothed leaves and broccoli-like buds that open to pink flowers that turn bronze as they dry. They remain attractive through the winter.

GARDEN USES Use low-growing sedums as groundcovers or edgings in sunny beds. They also look nice creeping over stone

retaining walls or spreading beside stone walks. Taller types are great in the middle of flower gardens. Combine them with 'Stella de Oro' daylily, yuccas, ornamental grasses, and blue, purple, or white asters. Try clumps of three or five in sunny open areas between shrubs.

GROWING AND PROPAGATION Plant in sun to light shade and average well-drained soil. Creeping types will also grow in partial shade. Taller types planted in fertile soil and shade may flop. To encourage 'Autumn Joy' to be self-supporting, pinch back growth in spring. Divide spreading forms as needed in spring or fall to control size. To increase your collection, divide plants or take stem cuttings anytime in summer.

'Autumn Joy' sedum makes a great early fall statement with its rounded, blue-tinged leaves and pink-blushed flowers.

Plant Profile

HARDINESS
Zones 3-9

SEASON OF BLOOM
Spring and summer

LIGHT REQUIREMENTS

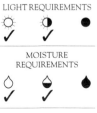

MOISTURE REQUIREMENTS

HEIGHT
2 inches - 2 feet

SPREAD
15 inches - 3 feet

Stokesia laevis
STOKES' ASTER

Plant drought-tolerant Stokes' asters in a well-drained sunny bed for soft color that lasts for weeks.

'Blue Danube' Stokes' aster is ideal for the front of a sunny border and makes a great cutting flower too.

APPEARANCE Stokes' asters have lavender, blue, or white flowers that look like standard aster flowers with a fluffy center. Flowers rise to 2 feet tall over a mound of long, slender leaves. They are pleasantly showy and bloom for months. 'Blue Danube' has blue flowers and reaches 15 inches tall. 'Klaus Jelitto' has big blue flowers and reaches 18 inches tall. 'Alba' has white flowers to 2 feet tall.

GARDEN USES Use Stokes' asters in the front or middle of a flower garden. Plant clusters of at least three plants of a single cultivar for the most attractive effect.

Blue Stokes' asters with orange coneflower (*Rudbeckia fulgida*) and violet sage (*Salvia* x *superba*) make a great long-blooming combination.

GROWING AND PROPAGATION Plant in sun and average, well-drained soil. To avoid root rots, the soil must be fast-draining even during wet winter months. Remove faded flowerheads from the plants periodically to encourage extended bloom. Plants seldom need division, but if you want to increase your supply of Stokes' asters, you can do so by lifting and dividing plants in the spring.

Plant Profile

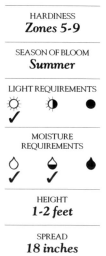

HARDINESS
Zones 5-9

SEASON OF BLOOM
Summer

LIGHT REQUIREMENTS

MOISTURE
REQUIREMENTS

HEIGHT
1-2 feet

SPREAD
18 inches

Tiarella spp.
FOAMFLOWER

Blanket a shady garden with the attractive lobed leaves and misty flower clusters of this native wildflower.

Allegheny foamflower offers frothy white spring flowers and fast-spreading foliage that turns a pretty red in the fall.

APPEARANCE Allegheny foamflower (*T. cordifolia*) has fuzzy spikes of small white or pastel pink flowers that arise over a rosette of maplelike leaves. The foliage remains attractive through the summer and turns red in fall. Allegheny foamflowers can spread into a handsome groundcover to 10 inches tall.

The hybrid cultivar 'Laird of Skye' has white flowers. 'Eco Running Tapestry' has red highlights on young leaves.

Wherry's foamflower (*T. wherryi*) looks similar to Allegheny foamflower but has pink flowers and forms a tidy clump that gradually increases in size over the years. In mild climates, the foliage turns red in winter.

GARDEN USES Foamflowers look wonderful with other spring-blooming wildflowers in a woodland garden. Try them in sweeps with snowdrop anemone (*Anemone sylvestris*), Dutchman's breeches (*Dicentra cucullaria*), and bloodroot (*Sanguinaria canadensis*) for a mix of white flowers of different shapes. You can also let Allegheny foamflowers creep across the front of any shady bed, including a flower garden or foundation planting. Foamflowers also look great with hostas and Japanese painted fern (*Athyrium goeringianum* 'Pictum').

GROWING AND PROPAGATION Plant foamflowers in partial to full shade and moist, rich, but well-drained soil. Irrigate during dry weather. Divide plants in spring or fall to limit their spread or to increase your supply of plants. Or, you can remove rooted runners from Allegheny foamflowers and replant them anytime during the growing season.

Plant Profile

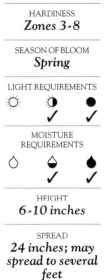

HARDINESS
Zones 3-8

SEASON OF BLOOM
Spring

LIGHT REQUIREMENTS
☼ ◐ ✓ ● ✓

MOISTURE REQUIREMENTS
◌ ◍ ✓ ● ✓

HEIGHT
6-10 inches

SPREAD
24 inches; may spread to several feet

Tulipa spp.
TULIP

*Try some species tulips as well as familiar hybrid tulips
for colorful and varied spring displays.*

**One of the
dainty species
tulips** you may
want to sample is
golden tulip
(*Tulipa
chrysantha*).

APPEARANCE Handsome six-petaled,
bowl-shaped flowers in yellow, red, pink,
white, orange, purple, and bicolors arise at
the top of slender stalks. Tulip species and
cultivars vary in shape, height, and bloom
time. Most types have broad, pointed
leaves. The following is only a small
sample of what's available for gardens.

T. tarda has narrow straplike leaves
and star-shaped white flowers with a
yellow center. It reaches only 4 inches tall.

Greigii tulips (*T. greigii*, varieties,
and hybrids) reach 12 inches tall, bloom
early to midseason, and have purple-
striped foliage. 'Red Riding Hood' is red;
'Corsage' is rose and yellow; 'Sweet Lady'
is apricot and off-white.

Fosteriana tulips (*T. fosteriana*,
varieties, and hybrids), also called

Emperor tulips, reach to 20 inches tall and
bloom early. They include 'Orange
Emperor', 'Red Emperor', and 'White
Emperor'.

Kaufmanniana tulips (*T.
kaufmanniana*, varieties, and hybrids) grow
to 8 inches tall and bloom very early. They
have stripes on the outside of the flower.
'Johann Strauss' is red and yellow; 'Pink
Dwarf' is scarlet and purple.

GARDEN USES Use tulips in informal
groups between perennials such as
cranesbills (*Geranium* spp.), peonies, and
daylilies. Plant seven, nine, or more of a
single cultivar per group to give an
impressive show. Choose early and
midseason cultivars for an extended
period of bloom. Try planting species
tulips with late-blooming daffodils and
early perennials.

GROWING AND PROPAGATION Plant
tulip bulbs in fall in a sunny site and
fertile, well-drained soil. The ideal site is
dry in summer and moist in spring and fall.
Species tulips can thrive for years. Hybrid
tulips bloom well only for a year or two.
After that, replant fresh bulbs. Remove
the foliage when it turns yellow. It's not
worth fertilizing hybrid tulips, but you can
scatter some bonemeal and cottonseed
meal around species tulips in spring.

Plant Profile

HARDINESS
Zones 3-8

SEASON OF BLOOM
Spring

LIGHT REQUIREMENTS
☀ ◐ ●
✓

MOISTURE
REQUIREMENTS
◊ ◖ ◆
✓ ✓

HEIGHT
4-30 inches

SPREAD
6-10 inches

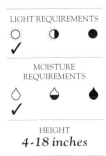

Verbena spp.

VERBENA

Let verbenas weave their way around and between other
sun-loving perennials to create a carpet of rich purple,
pink, or white flowers.

'Homestead Purple' verbena has masses of dazzling purple flowers that last from early summer until frost.

APPEARANCE Small tubular flowers that flare out into starry shapes appear in showy clusters through much of the growing season. The flowers arise at the end of stems covered in handsome, finely cut or lobed leaves.

Rose verbena (*V. canadensis*) is one of the hardiest verbenas. It reaches 18 inches tall with purple, pink, or white flowers and spreads to form a groundcover. 'Springbrook' has large rose flowers.

Moss verbena (*V. tenuisecta*; Zones 7 to 10) grows to 8 inches tall with prolific purple flower clusters.

There are several excellent hybrid cultivars. 'Homestead Purple' bears purple flowers the entire growing season. 'Old Royal Fragrance' is blue flowered and

aromatic. 'Snowball' is a white-flowered cultivar.

GARDEN USES Use creeping verbenas to edge sunny flower gardens or as a groundcover in sunny shrub beds. They also are great companions for taller perennials such as Japanese silver grass (*Miscanthus sinensis*), 'Powis Castle' artemisia, and black-eyed Susans (*Rudbeckia* spp.).

GROWING AND PROPAGATION Grow creeping verbenas in sun and average well-drained soil. Cut back lanky stems occasionally to keep the plants compact and encourage rebloom. To increase your collection, take stem cuttings anytime during the growing season.

Plant Profile

HARDINESS
Zones 4-10

SEASON OF BLOOM
Summer

LIGHT REQUIREMENTS
☼ ◑ ●
✓

MOISTURE REQUIREMENTS
◊ ◔ ●
✓

HEIGHT
4-18 inches

SPREAD
Can spread to several feet

Viola spp.
VIOLET

These demure cottage garden favorites can spread to cover large areas in light to full shade, forming a groundcover that's attractive long after the spring flowers fade.

Sweet violet blooms in early spring. The heart-shaped leaves spread to form an attractive groundcover.

Plant Profile

HARDINESS
Zones 3-9

SEASON OF BLOOM
Spring

LIGHT REQUIREMENTS
☀ ✓ ◑ ✓ ● ✓

MOISTURE REQUIREMENTS
◌ ◓ ✓ ◆ ✓

HEIGHT
1-12 inches

SPREAD
May spread to several feet

APPEARANCE Violet flowers have two upright petals and three spreading lower petals. Flowers may be white, blue, purple, or yellow, depending on the species. All have handsome heart-shaped leaves. Some grow in low clusters; others rise on weak stems.

Canada violet (*V. canadensis*; Zones 3 to 8) reaches 12 inches tall with white and yellow flowers.

Labrador violet (*V. labradorica*; Zones 3 to 8) stays low, to 8 inches tall, and has purple flowers. The variety *purpurea* has highly ornamental purple leaves.

Sweet violet (*V. odorata*; Zones 6 to 9) is a cottage garden favorite with fragrant flowers. 'White Czar' has white flowers with a yellow center. 'Royal Robe' has purple blossoms.

GARDEN USES Use violets to edge a shade or woodland garden. They look charming near lady fern (*Athyrium filix-femina*) and wildflowers such as wild blue phlox (*Phlox divaricata*). The foliage remains handsome long after the flowers are gone. You can also let violets form a groundcover beneath shrubs or around the base of tall perennials such as black snakeroot (*Cimicifuga racemosa*), Solomon's seals (*Polygonatum* spp.), and ferns.

GROWING AND PROPAGATION Plant in moist, rich, well-drained soil in light to full shade. Violets spread by creeping stems and by seed. You may need to transplant or weed out seedlings if they appear too prolifically. Divide in the spring or fall to control spread or to increase your collection of violets.

Yucca filamentosa
ADAM'S-NEEDLE, YUCCA

The bold daggerlike leaves and tall white flower spires of sturdy yucca plants accent softer perennials in a sunny garden.

Yucca has evergreen foliage that can withstand heat and dry conditions.

APPEARANCE Long spikes of white, bell-shaped flowers appear over rosettes of upright, sharp-tipped, swordlike leaves. The evergreen leaves are blue tinted and reach to 30 inches tall. The flower spikes may stretch to 5 feet or taller. 'Bright Edge' has gold-edged leaves and shorter flower spikes. 'Color Guard' has golden leaves with green margins.

GARDEN USES Use Adam's-needles for their bold form, interesting evergreen foliage, and durability in hot, dry sites. Mix them into flower gardens, shrub gardens, or sunny foundation plantings. They look good singly or in clusters of three. Try planting them with a surrounding carpet of moss phlox (*Phlox subulata*) and with bold companions such as ornamental grasses and black-eyed Susans (*Rudbeckia* spp.).

GROWING AND PROPAGATION Plant in sun to light shade and lean to average, well-drained soil. Water during prolonged drought. Remove faded flower stems to keep the plants tidy. Yuccas produce lateral shoots at the base of the plants. It's easy to remove and replant these offshoots to increase your collection.

Plant Profile

HARDINESS
Zones 3-10

SEASON OF BLOOM
Summer

LIGHT REQUIREMENTS
☼ ◐ ●
✓

MOISTURE REQUIREMENTS
◊ ◓ ◆
✓

HEIGHT
5-10 feet

SPREAD
3-6 feet

USDA Plant Hardiness Zone Map

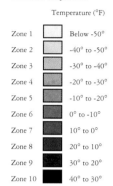

Average annual
minimum temperature

Temperature (°F)

Zone 1		Below -50°
Zone 2		-40° to -50°
Zone 3		-30° to -40°
Zone 4		-20° to -30°
Zone 5		-10° to -20°
Zone 6		0° to -10°
Zone 7		10° to 0°
Zone 8		20° to 10°
Zone 9		30° to 20°
Zone 10		40° to 30°

SOURCES

Plants and Seeds

Busse Gardens
5873 Oliver Ave. SW
Cokato, MN 55321

The Daffodil Mart
7463 Heath Tr.
Gloucester, VA 23061

Garden Place
P.O. Box 388
6780 Heisley Rd.
Mentor, OH 44060

Klehm Nursery
4210 N. Duncan Rd.
Champaign, IL 61821

Milaeger's Gardens
4838 Douglas Ave.
Racine, WI 53402–2498

Niche Gardens
1111 Dawson Rd.
Chapel Hill, NC 27516

Old House Gardens
536 Third St.
Ann Arbor, MI
48103–4957
Offers heirloom tulips

Prairie Nursery, Inc.
P.O. Box 306
Westfield, WI 53964
*Seeds and plants of prairie
wildflowers*

John Scheepers Inc.
23 Tulip Dr.
Bantam, CT 06750

Shady Oaks Nursery
112 10th Ave. SE
Waseca, MN 56093
*Specializes in plants for
shade*

Wayside Gardens
1 Garden Ln.
Hodges, SC 29695–0001

White Flower Farm
Litchfield, CT 06759

Garden Supplies and Equipment

Gardener's Supply Co.
128 Intervale Rd.
Burlington, VT 05401

Gardens Alive!
5100 Schenley Pl.
Lawrenceburg, IN 47025

Harmony Farm Supply
P.O. Box 460
Graton, CA 95444

**Peaceful Valley Farm
Supply**
P.O. Box 2209
Grass Valley, CA 95945

RECOMMENDED READING

Burrell, C. Colston.
Ferns. Brooklyn, N.Y.:
Brooklyn Botanic
Garden, 1994.

Curtis, Will C.
Propagation of Wildflowers.
Revised by William E.
Brumback. Framingham,
Mass.: New England
Wildflower Society, 1996.

Ellis, Barbara W., and
Fern Marshall Bradley,
eds. *The Organic
Gardener's Handbook of
Natural Insect and Disease
Control.* Emmaus, Pa.:
Rodale Press, 1992.

Greenlee, John.
*The Encyclopedia of
Ornamental Grasses.*
Emmaus, Pa.: Rodale
Press, 1992.

Martin, Deborah L., and
Grace Gershuny, eds. *The
Rodale Book of
Composting.* Emmaus, Pa.:
Rodale Press, 1992.

McClure, Susan. *The
Herb Gardener: A Guide
for All Seasons.* Pownal,
Vt.: Storey
Communications, 1995.

McClure, Susan, and
C. Colston Burrell.
*Rodale's Successful Organic
Gardening: Perennials.*
Emmaus, Pa.: Rodale
Press, 1993.

McKeon, Judith C.
The Encyclopedia of Roses.
Emmaus, Pa.: Rodale
Press, 1995.

Pettingill, Amos.
*The White Flower Farm
Garden Book.* Litchfield,
Conn.: White Flower
Farm, 1995.

Phillips, Ellen, and C.
Colston Burrell. *Rodale's
Illustrated Encyclopedia of
Perennials.* Emmaus, Pa.:
Rodale Press, 1993.

Taylor's Guide Staff.
*Taylor's Guide to Ground
Covers, Vines & Grasses.*
Boston: Houghton Mifflin
Co., 1987.

Tufts, Craig, and Peter
Loewer. *The National
Wildlife Federation's Guide
to Gardening for Wildlife.*
Emmaus, Pa.: Rodale
Press, 1995.

INDEX

Page numbers in *italics* refer
to illustrations and photographs

CREDITS

Susan McClure is an author, lecturer, and garden designer from Valparaiso, Indiana.
She has written several gardening books, including *Successful Organic Gardening: Perennials*.

Bobbie Schwartz is a landscape consultant and designer and the owner of Bobbie's Green Thumb in Shaker Heights, Ohio.
She also gives lectures on landscape use of perennials and ornamental grasses.

Robin Siktberg is a garden designer and horticulturist with a special interest in perennials.
She is also a freelance writer, lecturer, and photographer and lives in Chesterland, Ohio.

Alexander Apanius is a horticulturist and landscape designer and the owner
of Alexander A. Apanius, Inc., of Hudson, Ohio. He is the former director of the Cleveland Botanical Garden.

Photographic Credits

Key: *a* = above   *b* = below   *c* = center   *l* = left   *r* = right

Defenders Ltd 90; Alan and Linda Detrick © 1996 ALD photo inc 44*r*, 94, 105, 118, 119, 123, 129, 144; Garden Matters 72*c*;
Hozelock plc 82; Jerry Pavia 8, 21, 33*b*, 37, 44*l*, 48, 49*a*, 54*b*, 56, 59, 66, 68 *l c*, 95, 97, 98, 100, 101, 102, 104, 106, 108, 109,
113, 114, 117, 122, 125, 126, 127, 128, 130, 132, 133, 135, 137, 138, 139, 140, 141, 146, 147, 148, 150, 151, 153; Joanne Pavia
99, 152; Photo/Nats Inc. 149 (Liz Ball), 60, 120 (Gay Bumgarner), 116 (Robert E. Lyons), 134 (Ann Reilly); Positive Images 7
(Margaret Hensel), 15 (Pam Spaulding), 33*a* (Harry Haralambou), 45, 80, 91*a* (Patricia J. Bruno), 49*b*, 70*b*, 89, 111 (Jerry
Howard), 54*a*, 70*a* (Les Campbell), 74*b* (Lee Lockwood), 78, 110 (Karen Bussolini), 91 *ac* (Jacob Mosser); Rodale Stock Images
69*r*, 76, 77, 91*bc*; Bobbie Schwartz 96; Robin A. Siktberg 74*a*, 103, 107, 112, 115, 131, 142; Harry Smith Horticultural
Photographic Collection 31, 72*a* & *b*, 83, 121, 124, 136, 145; Peter Stiles 13, 42, 143; Juliette Wade 2; Bob Woods 57.

All other photographs are the copyright of Quarto Inc.

While every effort has been made to acknowledge copyright holders, Quarto would like to
apologize should any omissions have been made.